ISSUES IN
SOCIALIST⎯⎯⎯⎯
⎯⎯⎯⎯ECONOMIC
MODERNIZATION

ISSUES IN SOCIALIST_____ _____ECONOMIC MODERNIZATION

Jan S. Prybyla

PRAEGER

PRAEGER SPECIAL STUDIES • PRAEGER SCIENTIFIC

Library of Congress Cataloging in Publication Data

Prybyla, Jan S
    Issues in Socialist economic modernization.

    Bibliography: p.
    Includes index.
    1. Marxian economics. 2. Communist countries
--Economic policy. I. Title.
HB97.5.P895   335.4'13   80-18647
ISBN 0-03-057 962-7

Published in 1980 by Praeger Publishers
CBS Educational and Professional Publishing
A Division of CBS, Inc.
521 Fifth Avenue, New York, New York 10017 U.S.A.

0123456789 145 987654321

Printed in the United States of America

FOREWORD
Ray S. Cline

In this unusual and thought-provoking scholarly inquiry, Jan Prybyla presents an accurate picture of the fundamentally flawed Soviet economic system, in which overrigid controls from the top and lack of incentives at the bottom cause many inadequacies and frequent serious failures.

What is more remarkable, Professor Prybyla makes a careful comparison of the Soviet economy with the Chinese Communist model. While the leaders and bureaucrats in China spring from a radically different cultural source, they have in general copied the original Stalinist model of economic structure and are likely to find it subject to the same inherent defects. Its future development, despite China's modernization policy, is still subject to many uncertainties. Moreover, China is still feeling the disastrous effects of Mao Zedong's effort in the Cultural Revolution to escape from the Soviet bureaucratic system of management and has had little opportunity to introduce its own modifications to the Soviet economic model now being restored by Deng Xiaoping.

As if this analysis of the two giant Communist nations did not already provide an impressively broad scope, two other variants on the Soviet-type economy are also examined: Hungary—within the Soviet sphere where the emphasis is on foreign trade—and its attempts to experiment with a market economy; and Yugoslavia with its worker councils—a Marxist-Leninist economy excluded from the Soviet bloc. Professor Prybyla ably demonstrates both the innovations that countries can undertake under the system and the limitations they encounter at its margins. His description of the Yugoslav economy is particularly timely, as many observers wonder what course post-Tito Yugoslavia will take.

Professor Prybyla's emphasis on the underemployment of both people and resources in the Soviet-type economies and the suppressed inflation that results are of interest to strategic analysts of comparative world power. Of even greater interest is his basic thesis that the Soviet-type economy in all its guises is not an effective vehicle for modernization. In his view, modernization demands high levels of research and technology, innovation, productivity, and capital investment. It also demands a set of attitudes on the part of the regime toward its own programs: a willingness to make changes, to admit errors, to take risks, and to remember "that economies exist to promote the physical welfare of their members." The last item requires providing incomes and rewards that deal fairly with the members of the system according to their performance and their intrinsic individual worth, giving them a voice in the shaping of their environment rather than imposing "institutionalized subservience and docility." Unfortunately, the Russians have had no historical experience of democracy in any sphere and in the foreseeable future are unlikely to experiment with change, unless the widening gap between the system's promises and its performance creates unbearable strains.

The Georgetown Center for Strategic and International Studies is pleased to present such a broad-gauged piece of scholarship so competently done.

Executive Director
World Power Studies
Center for Strategic and International
  Studies, Georgetown University
Washington, D.C.

March 1980

PREFACE

This book grew out of my interest in China's decision, taken early in 1977, to pursue vigorously the objective of modernizing the economy, now that the alleged Maoist obstacles to modernization have been removed. My study of Maoism as an economic system—a "left" deviation from the Soviet prototype first fashioned by Stalin in the 1930s and reformed by Stalin's successors in the 1960s—prompted me to ask: How far down the road to modernization can the Chinese go by simply following in the steps of the Russians, without bumping into serious problems that are built into the contemporary ("modern") Soviet system? The study of China's experience (Chapter 2) suggests rather conclusively that some of the difficulties that China experienced under Mao in pulling the economy out of its backwardness, and which, in the wake of the disgrace of the "Gang of Four," were attributed to Mao's economic folklore and policy, were really not Maoist at all but rather organic parts of the Soviet-type economic system. China under Mao remained a member of the Soviet systemic family. There were, of course, many modifications in areas such as goal-setting; the emphasis put on, and meaning given to, self-reliance; the nature and mechanism of motivation; and the way innovation was sought and planning conducted. Some of these modifications (traceable for the most part to the Great Leap Forward and Cultural Revolution periods) were deep and pervasive. They did not, however, add up to a clear-cut break with the Soviet-type system. When the modernizers returned in China, despite the continued verbal hostility toward the Soviet Union, the initial steps taken to change the institutions of the economy looked like steps leading in the direction of the contemporary Soviet-type institutional structure. The Maoist left deviation was, for the time being, corrected by pushing the economy to the "right," that is, in a Soviet direction. Symptomatically, the party and state apparat men, a multitude of them, began to creep out of the holes in the ground to which they had been relegated by Mao's left-wing allies and, hesitantly at first, began to govern and plan as they once had been wont to. The average age of the top leadership, the temperamental and professional predispositions of the bureaucratic hordes, and the whole philosophical tenor of the country, deeply shaken by decades of recurring ideological upheavals, would seem to stack the odds against any daredevil systemic leaps; yet one can never tell. If the leaders take the comparatively easy way out and simply modernize à la russe, using the Soviet precedent as guide and Soviet-type institutions (which are in place, although in bad disrepair) as instruments of modernization, they may find new troubles and burdens piling up on top of the old ones. This is so because despite spectacular achievements on high-priority, narrow fronts, the Soviet-type economy in its contemporary form is not a good vehicle of economic modernization. Not the least of its problems is the high moral price paid for the little modernity that manages to filter down from the defense sector to the masses of workers and consumers.

Some of the organic problems of the contemporary Soviet-type economy are examined at length in Chapter 1. The reforms that the Soviets introduced in the 1960s to transform the old Stalinist administrative machine into an engine of intensive growth (and perhaps even of consumer welfare) were very conservative. They never touched the guts of the system, concentrating on plastic surgery of the face-lifting variety. The goal-setting, information, coordination, and motivation structures of the Soviet economy are not significantly different today from what they were before the changes. Some East European economists refer to the Soviet reforms as "nonreforms," and they are right in the sense that the basic principles and procedures of the Stalinist economy were not disturbed by the alterations carried out in the 1960s. This view is not to deny that a great deal of sophisticated and ground-breaking work was and continues to be done on the theoretical plane. However, theoretical constructs get translated into systemic practice exceedingly slowly, if at all. As the dominant power—at least on its Western flank—the Soviet Union sets the pace of systemic reforms for the countries of Eastern Europe. China is not bound by this constraint. Its decision on how far to go in transforming the economic system inherited from the Soviets without sacrificing socialist values will be of historic interest.

About the same time that the Soviets were making administrative alterations to the Stalinist command structure, the Hungarians—and for a time the Czechs—went further. Conceptually, they crossed the politically sensitive line and drew up a scheme for a rather thorough systemic reform. The vertically structured command economy was to be rebuilt in a more horizontally inclined direction. The proposed decentralization was to be truly "economic," that is, rooted in commercial, contractual relations among independent economic units, these relations being established in accordance with information provided by a freed price system. The state planners were to concentrate on macroeconomic magnitudes—the strategic proportions and directions of the economy—and they were to communicate their preferences to economic units primarily by indirect, manipulative fiscal and monetary means rather than by direct physical orders. The Hungarian reforms proposed to transform a centrally planned, administratively commanded economy into a guided market economy. The underlying ideas were not all that different from those associated with the earlier Yugoslav systemic revolution. They were, however, couched in more circumspect language and skirted the thorny issue of enterprise management by workers.

Although, as elsewhere, reformist ideas in Hungary outran reform acts, the implementation of the theoretical reform guidelines went further than in the Soviet Union. Central determination of output targets for enterprises was abolished, compulsory delivery quotas for collective farms were done away with, commercial contracts among enterprises were not only permitted but encouraged, creating in essence the preconditions for "planning from below" (that is, up from market relations). Some prices were freed completely, some others were freed in part, the separation of domestic from foreign markets was reduced through the introduction of more realistic exchange rates and state foreign trade corporations were demoted to the rank of commission agents for enterprises. Private-sector activities related to the provision of all kinds of consumer services were no longer discriminated against.

The problem with systemic reforms is that they must be comprehensive and, at least in theory, should be introduced at once. Politically this is often not feasible. So, in Hungary too, the reforms were only partial and they came in hesitant stages. Numerous institutional "brakes" on the marketization of the economy were retained and grew over time as external balance-of-payments difficulties multipled and internal pressures mounted. By 1974 much of the original reform had been undone, and the commitment to it had been weakened both within the party and among sections of the working class.

It is the argument of this book that economic modernization means something more than up-to-date technology, high-factor productivity, a fast rate of innovation, and generous capital endowment per worker. These "objective" attributes of modernization are dependent variables, so to speak. They depend on a set of "subjective" attributes that concern the relationship of the individual person to his immediate working environment and to the more distant total economic system in which he and his workshop are integrated. The thesis argued in the first three chapters is that the attainment and viability of the first ("objective") set of attributes turns on the (at least partial) achievement of the second set of "subjective" or attitudinal attributes. The latter require what is broadly described as economic decentralization: the structuring of the system's goal-setting, information, and coordination mechanisms in a horizontal direction. In simpler language, the individual economic unit must be granted considerable latitude to make its own decisions and either benefit from them or pay a penalty for the mistakes it makes. The autonomy of the individual economic unit (consumer, worker, enterprise) does not preclude intervention by the public authority at the economy's macro level in behalf of the collective interest: but such intervention, it is argued, should be in the nature of indirect manipulative guidance rather than direct command. Direct orders, especially at the micro level, are occasionally necessary; but they should be the exception and not the rule.

An influential body of economic thought holds that, in the past, the autonomy of individual economic units, when granted, always stopped short of the enterprise in question. Whatever the system—market or administrative command—economic decentralization was thought of in terms of arrangements enabling enterprises and consumers to take meaningful allocative decisions without too much outside interference. Autonomy of the individual in his capacity as worker was seen as being achieved through an intermediary process in one of two ways. The worker took meaningful allocative decisions as regards his income flow through his trade union representatives and the collective bargaining process; and he expressed his buying preferences through his income-spending pattern in the market. (Soviet-type administrative command systems severely limit both expressions). Critics of this procedure argue that for a market autonomy to be solidly based and complete, there is need to provide the worker <u>qua</u> worker with specific institutional means of directly expressing his preferences regarding the conditions under which he works. In other words, there is need for worker participation in the management of enterprises. Such participation or codetermination would overcome, so goes the argument, the alienation of workers from their work, their workshops, and the system. It would democratize the system by extending the give-and-take of the market to procedures internal to the firm. The worker would no longer be mutilated as a human being by being treated as a mechanical factor of production.

A number of theories of worker codetermination have been developed in recent decades. In Chapter 4 one of the more comprehensive ones is outlined, together with arguments advanced both for and against it. Some economists argue that Yugoslavia has tried to implement a labor-managed, market-oriented system, generally along such conceptual lines. An account of this experiment is given in the second part of the chapter. Yugoslavia's most notable contribution to the problems examined in this book is not, I think, the marketization of a Soviet-type administrative command economy, but the deliberate extension of the market principle to the structure of the firm. That is why Chapter 4 concentrates on the institutions of worker participation in enterprise management rather than reviewing the whole makeup of Yugoslav market socialism.

Chapter 5 summarizes the major findings and draws some conclusions from the Soviet-type administrative command system's quest for economic modernization.

CONTENTS

ISSUES IN SOCIALIST____ ____ECONOMIC MODERNIZATION

1
ECONOMIC MODERNIZATION AND THE CONTEMPORARY SOVIET-TYPE ECONOMY

THE SEARCH FOR MODERNIZATION

Many developing countries—socialist and nonsocialist, planned and unplanned—are looking for a workable model of economic modernization. Among the more prominent searchers is the People's Republic of China. In the most synthetic terms modernization means intensive growth, that is, growth based on improvements in factor productivity rather than on simple additions of factors.

To developing Marxist-Leninist countries, but to others as well, the contemporary Soviet-type economy offers itself as just such an effective vehicle of modernization. To those who embrace the Marxist-Leninist creed, from Angola and Mozambique to Cuba and Vietnam, it offers the guarantee of faith, the convenience of staying within the broad framework of administrative central planning (which obviates the agony of making systemic choices), and an impressive record of achievement. In the Ninth Five-Year Plan (1971-1975), after the installation of various modernizing reforms, the updated Stalinist economy of the Soviet Union increased its industrial production volume by 43 percent (8.6 percent a year), its consumer goods output by 37 percent (7.4 percent a year), and its farm output by 13 percent (2.6 percent a year) despite exceptionally adverse weather conditions. Much of this growth, it is claimed, came from improvements in labor productivity. In industry the productivity of labor rose by 34 percent (6.8 percent a year) and in agriculture by 22 percent (4.4 percent a year). At the same time wages and salaries went up by 20 percent (4 percent a year) and per capita real income by 24 percent (4.8 percent a year). Military capability has been raised to awesome heights and the influence of the Soviet Union in Africa and other sensitive places has been

1

significantly extended and consolidated. There was stability of employment, no joblessness, and no overt inflation. The security of individuals has been improved through larger outlays on social welfare. Popular discontent with this or that aspect of the system was kept within politically tolerable and manageable bounds. More of the same is expected in the current (1976-1980) plan. The Soviet Union, it is argued, has been well served by its contemporary economic system. The system is available, more or less free of charge, to anyone willing to give it a try.

The big stakes right now are in China's choice. Having shed many of its Maoist accretions, the Chinese economy stands at a crossroads. Despite Peking's verbal abuse of the Soviets and all their works, the post-Mao Chinese economy is today closer to the contemporary Soviet-type model than it has been at any time after 1965. The kinship, of course, has been there all along. Now that the Maoist additions to a basically Soviet-type system have been removed, the question is whether further institutional changes will be in the contemporary Soviet direction or in a different one. My purpose here is to see if the rejuvenated Soviet-type economy (rejuvenated in the Soviet Union by the adjustments of the late 1950s and the 1960s) contains obstacles to modernization. After all, if China and other countries choose to move in the direction of contemporary Soviet-type economic institutions, it is not without interest to ask whether these institutions will do the job expected of them.

ECONOMIC MODERNIZATION

The definition of modernization as intensive growth is clearly insufficient. I think modernization and a "modern" economy mean the simultaneous presence in society of two sets of things: a set of largely technical or "objective" attributes and a set of attitudes. There is bound to be less controversy about the first list than the second.

The objective attributes of modernization are four in number: high levels of education, research, science, and technology; a high rate of innovation; a high factor productivity; and a high level of capital endowment per worker.

The subjective or attitudinal attributes include the following: a widespread preference for and capacity to absorb change; a scientific outlook marked by intellectual flexibility and the willingness to admit demonstrated error; a readiness and capacity to take risks and assume responsibility; a democratization of human relations that—while it does not exclude the exercise of authority, presence of hierarchical relationships, and discipline—implies: that people are judged equitably in light of their intrinsic worth as persons and by their professional performance, the absence of institutionalized subservience and docility, and participation, or the presence of institutional means designed to associate people in the shaping of the social (and, more narrowly, working) environment; and a recognition that the raison d'être of any economic system is to cater to user wants, that is, that economies exist to promote the physical welfare of their members—a desideratum that includes not only the provision of private and collective goods and services but also the elimination of the grosser kind of income and power disparities.

Obviously no economy can score 100 percent on each of the nine attributes. At the very least, however, there should be built into the system's institutions a propensity to encourage and nurture such attributes.

I would argue that it is possible for a country to possess several of the technical requisites of modernization without having anything like the full range of the behavioral attributes. The latest science and technology, know-how, and capital equipment can be nowadays imported en masse if you are fortunate to have oil under your feet. The presence of one set of attributes without the other gives rise to social disequilibrium. Modernization in such circumstances rests on shifting, unstable foundations; it is both dangerous and illusory.

SOVIET-TYPE ECONOMY

It is useful to distinguish between the original Soviet-type economy conceived and implemented by Stalin and the contemporary revised version of the original used by the Soviets and some others. The original Stalinist economy can be described as a closed multi-level supercorporation that owns the bulk of society's natural resources and capital, is administratively directed from the center by a unified management for purposes mandated by the management, and is closely integrated with the state and the communist monoparty.[1] The important elements are: the centralization of decisions; administrative, directive planning that uses primarily physical techniques of planning and relies heavily on politically induced objectives and criteria of performance; the social ownership of natural and produced resources with very narrow property rights vested in the actual users of those resources (enterprise managements); the primacy of domestic economic issues over foreign trade (that is, stress on capital accumulation from domestic sources); and the close integration of the economic system with the political and ideological state and party apparatus.

The Stalinist model was used in the Soviet Union and Eastern Europe (except Yugoslavia) to promote rapid growth of the extensive type until some time after the death of Stalin. It was modified in the 1960s in order to enable the economy to set out on the path of intensive growth. While it would be inaccurate to describe the modifications as cosmetic, they certainly stopped far short of thorough systemic reform. Of all the bloc reforms, those in the Soviet Union were among the more conservative. The contemporary Soviet-type economy can be described, therefore, as a multilevel supercorporation that owns the bulk of society's natural resources and capital, is administratively directed from the center by a selectively decentralized management for purposes mandated by the management, and is closely integrated with the state and the communist monoparty. The important elements are: the centralization of decisions; administrative, directive, selectively decentralized planning that uses a mixture of physical and financial planning techniques and a mixture of politically induced and economically derived objectives and criteria; the social ownership of natural and produced resources with fairly narrow property rights vested in the actual users of those resources (enterprise managements); the significant role of foreign trade in promoting domestic technological change (that is, a semiopen economy); and the close integration with the political and ideological state and party apparats.

Compared with the Stalinist original, the contemporary Soviet-type economy selectively delegates decision-making responsibilities to lower-level authorities, without, however, abandoning the principle of high-level centralization of basic macroeconomic goal formulation and microeconomic output and input norm setting. Perhaps more importantly, there appears to be more group bargaining at the center and more inclination to listen to opinions expressed by lower echelons of the economic pyramid. While the economy continues to be administratively commanded from the center, financial ("economic," "law of value") indicators are given more prominence than in earlier times. Profitability, for example, has come to be regarded as a key criterion of enterprise performance, and economic accountability (khozraschet, that is, the enterprise's responsibility to cover its costs out of its revenues) has been made more feasible through a wholesale price reform and extended to cover collective farms. Prices continue to be set by the center, but they reflect branch average production costs more accurately than before. The bulk of capital and natural resources is owned by the supercorporation as in the old days, and property rights vested in the actual users of these factors (enterprise managements) have not been significantly enlarged. Finally, while foreign trade is still insulated from the internal price structure, it is no longer seen as a mere appendage to domestic plans—it has come to play an important role in promoting technological modern- ization of the domestic economy and, vis-a-vis East European countries, is regarded by many Soviet planners as one of the more effective means of eventual regional economic integration.

I shall examine the main features of the contemporary Soviet- type economy, some of which represent, in my opinion, systemic problems in the way of economic modernization. The issues will be dealt with under five headings: goal formulation, self-reliance, motivation, innovation, and planning.

GOAL FORMULATION

"Goal formulation" means the process of defining societal objectives (social preference functions)—both functional and sec- toral. The basic features of this process in a contemporary Soviet- type economy are summarized in the following sections.

Absence of a Built-in Social Goal Formulation Mechanism

A fundamental feature of the system is the absence of any built-in mechanism of social goal formulation, that is, there is no institutional means for revealing—automatically, spontaneously, on an ongoing basis—what needs to be done in society. In "marketless socialism," as it is sometimes called, society's objectives have to be constructed consciously, deliberately, and administratively by someone with the political clout to do the job: the political leader- ship, speaking through the "planners" (the dominant participants in the system), and served by a goal-setting bureaucracy.

In modernization, a major problem caused by the systemic need to define deliberately societal goals is conservatism in the sense of a lack of get-up-and-go. There are at least two reasons for that lack. The first concerns the goal-setting bureaucracy it- self; the second the goal-setting techniques used by that bureaucracy.

The goal-setting process calls for a very sizable and com- plex administrative apparatus. The fixing of social objectives manually at both the macro and micro levels is a gigantic under- taking that grows larger and more difficult as the economy expands. Practice shows that the bureaucracy responsible for translating the top leadership's highly aggregated targets into operational objectives proliferates in rough conformity with the Parkinsonian law; it is huge, unwieldy, vested in its interests, and is, furthermore, prone to jurisdictional overlaps and duplication. Finally, like all bureaucracies, it is routine bound and averse to risks.

Because of the magnitude of the task and the informational problems posed, the usual technique has been to look at reported past results, add to these a percentage, and by this simple process arrive at new objectives. This "ratchet" technique has had, as we shall see, unfortunate repercussions on the behavior of those executing the goals.[2] However, our main interest for the moment is with the conservatism inherent in a technique for formulating future objectives that relies inordinately on a quick study of the past.

Centralization of Goal Formulation

In the contemporary Soviet-type economy basic societal goals are determined in highly aggregated form by an inner group of political leaders on the basis of information supplied to the group from the field by the planning apparatus. (The goals are subsequently translated by the same planning bureaucracy into specific operational targets.)

The rationale for the centralization of goal-setting is found in the Marxist theory of cognition, the Leninist theory and practice of the Communist Party as vanguard, and the self-interest of the self-purging, self-coopting ruling oligarchy.

For the Soviet-type economy administrative centralization of goal formulation is not just a procedure; it is an objective in itself. "The whole rationale of the Soviet command system is a belief that the central planners could make better decisions for enterprises than they would make themselves in the pursuit of profit."[3]

The fact that centralized goal formulation is itself an objective of the system, and a very important one at that, means active avoidance—not to say abhorrence—of spontaneity, diversity, competition, and autonomy of the individual conscience. Thus the system is deprived of the potential benefits that could flow from presently suppressed ability; it makes for ossification and generally runs counter to the attitudinal requisites of economic modernization. It encourages arrogant elites, class differentiation, and—contrary to the announced purpose of diffusing decision-making power—creeping recentralization.

Mandatory Nature of Goals

The social goals set by the center are mandatory, not indicative; they are direct, specific orders—with name and address attached—not general suggestions. The contemporary Soviet-type economy is, like its Stalinist predecessor, a command economy.

The mandatory nature of goals as well as the detail in which the goals are cast both accentuate a problem common to all economic systems: the possibility of conflict between the social good and the preferences of individual economic units. In a market economy the price information received by economic units (firms, consumers, workers) is (horizontal) pure information to which the recipient adapts as he chooses. There is in such a setting a flexibility that is absent in a system of specific orders. Where "the interests of the enterprise and that of society" do not mesh, enterprise behavior (and the same applies to workers and consumers) becomes distorted relative to the planners' expressed wishes. Orders are carried out "formalistically." Contrary to Marx, the incidence of conflict appears to be greater under socialism than under its capitalist predecessor. The conflict, moreover, has very distinct class overtones, and because of the superior-subordinate nature of the economic relationship it tends to become antagonistic rather quickly.

Number and Detail of Goals

A feature of the Soviet-type economy is the proliferation of instructions issued by the center, ranging from broad macrosocial magnitudes to minute, not to say trivial, microeconomic detail. The macrosocial magnitudes include: targets for the rate of GNP growth broken down into sectoral and industry growth rates; allocation of national product to consumption and investment with specification of shares going to national defense; size of the labor force; scope and rate of technical change; direct rationing of key inputs; location of industry; and so on. The economy's basic production and other units (enterprises or associations of enterprises) receive about a dozen strategic success indicators, which include the volume and assortment of output of the most important products, sales volume, profit and profitability, and total wages fund.

From the standpoint of modernization several undesirable results follow. Here we note only what at the time of the reforms was referred to as "petty tutelage," the smothering of grassroots initiative by the central authority's contradictory and often unworkable directives. The center cannot possibly know all or even most of what needs to be done at the bottom of the heap. It follows that many of the orders it issues are busywork that merely add extra cost to the system's already formidable information bill.

Ranking of Goals ("Goal Discontinuities")

The Soviet-type economy ranks its planner-determined goals in a sharply differentiated order of priorities. In the Stalinist system the ranking—from top to bottom—ranged from primary indicators that received favored treatment in every respect to exploitative ones such as collective farm delivery quotas and procurement prices. In the contemporary Soviet-type economy the range is from solicitous affection to benign neglect. The ranking of goals involves an either-or rather than a more-or-less approach with regard to the primary indicators (100 percent fulfillment = bliss; 99 percent fulfillment = woe); sharp breaks between objectives; and an imbalanced, selective growth of the economy. The way goals are ranked in the Soviet-type economy—at both the macro and micro levels—follows naturally from both the difficulty of establishing for the economy as a whole a system of simultaneous equations that would yield a system of balanced objectives, and the impossibility of fulfilling all the planner's objectives. Failure may result from shortage of the required inputs, incompatible goals, or from a variety of other cogent reasons. In such circumstances the planners must indicate clearly which goals are considered to be really important and which may be sacrificed or underachieved (the latter are known as "buffers" or "shock absorbers").

The current approach produces sharp contrasts in the economy's level of development among sectors, industries, firms, and even within firms (for example, as between production and auxiliary operations), as well as jerky adjustments in the operation of the economy and its constituent units.

Time Horizons

Theoretically the Soviet-type centrally planned economy is geared to the formulation of broad long-term goals translated into investment decisions reaching out over five and more years. Indeed, a major advantage of the centrally planned economy, cited by its proponents, is precisely this ability to grasp the future, bend it to the collective will, and avoid randomness. The system, it is argued, eliminates the unpredictability and anarchy of scattered individual decisions and thereby assures smooth growth.

In practice things are different. The Soviet-type economy is operationally oriented toward the short run; in fact, toward the execution of the current, immediate tasks at hand. The main reason is that the performance of economic units under the plan is evaluated and rewarded or punished primarily by reference to short-run output and other primary targets ("success indicators"). The annual plan and its quarterly subdivisions is the plan in terms of benefits and costs to the executors; it is replete with details that bring in immediate rewards or cause trouble. The system has an inbuilt bias in favor of near horizons. For the grassroots and intermediate echelon operators of the system (managers and their hierarchical supervisors up to and including the ministerial bureaucracies), the longer-range time scale involves tangible psychological diseconomies.[4] In sum, there is both a sharp rank-ordering of functional goals and time horizons in an all-or-nothing order.

The systemic propensity to actually (not rhetorically) discount the future gives rise, in a longer-range perspective, to a wasteful use of scarce resources. It tends also to underemphasize pure research (especially as this relates to the achievement of lower-level goals) and to focus on rather narrow, highly applied innovation carrying immediate payoffs.

Tautness

A key principle of Soviet-type central administrative planning is tautness, that is, the maximization of planned output goals with a concurrent minimization of planned inputs and inventories. The purpose is to use resources fully and most effectively.[5] The results, however, do not appear to be in conformity with the planners' intent.

The scenario unfolds roughly as follows: From experience, enterprise managers know that the center will demand output performance based on its judgment of what needs to be done (overall goals) and what the individual enterprise can do (that is, what inputs are required). The enterprise's capacity to influence the center's decisions regarding output and input goals depends to an important degree on the enterprise's precise location on the planners' scale of sectoral, industrial, and other preferences. This capacity to influence, while greater than in the past, is still marginal. Experience has taught that, despite assurances to the contrary, the enterprise's output plan will be subject to frequent planner- or party-mandated upward changes before its completion. Normally these changes will not be accompanied by increases in inputs. The changes are due to a variety of causes: altered

domestic or international conditions, changes in planners' perceptions, and jurisdictional confusions (especially between governmental and party organs), to mention only the most important ones.

Four general results—not intended by the planners—follow
from the system's devotion to tautness: misleading information;
high information costs; chronic shortages; and "empire building."
These results occur as follows:

The information supplied to the center by the periphery tends
to be misleading. Specifically, enterprises (often with the backing
of their branch ministries) try to secure a "soft" plan, one that can
easily be fulfilled and that leaves room for contingencies such as a
sudden upping of the output plan. Wrong information—made possible
by the center's inability to check out every report it receives from
the field—normally takes three simultaneous forms: understate-
ment of enterprise capacity to turn out output, overstatement of input needs, and hoarding of labor and capital just in case (the so-
called "hidden reserves" that the system is constantly uncovering,
but that hide again as soon as they are discovered). The net effect
of resorting to precautionary hoarding (the hedge factor) is the opposite of that intended, that is, underemployment of inputs especially of labor and capital; in simple language, waste. This, of course,
has an adverse effect on the key ingredient of economic modernization: labor and capital productivity.

The chronic presence of faulty information in the system is,
of course, known to everyone concerned. It creates an atmosphere
of all-round distrust and suspicion not conducive to the orderly and
comradely conduct of affairs. Ideally, under the socialist system
and the regime of almost universal public property in the means of
production, information should be freely and willingly shared and
widely diffused. In practice the opposite is the case. The result is
very high cost of information gathering, transmittal, and processing. The information supplied from the field has to be monitored
and verified by a host of supervisory and auditing authorities with
overlapping rights and competing loyalties. The execution of orders
has similarly to be checked and rechecked. The supervisory agencies themselves have to be supervised. The list is endless.

The principle of taut planning (plus disequilibrium pricing)
creates an economy of chronic shortages, a permanent sellers' market. An economy of scarcity (not limited to consumers' goods only)
gives rise to black markets and bureaucratic corruption (bribery,
on-the-side payments, barter favors). Black markets and a cor-
rupted bureaucracy lead to two major results, the first psychological,
the second economic. The psychological results are widespread
cynicism, disbelief, hypocrisy, and large credibility gaps that do

little to enhance the legitimacy of the system in the eyes of participants. [6] In addition to other disappointments, there is the failure of a dream. All this makes it difficult for the system to pose as the moral wave of the future. Economically, the results are: bribery and other under-the-counter payments and "unilateral transfers from the state to individuals" (theft) that give rise to changes in the planned distribution of income without any corresponding increase in output; the creation of unreported income and output from extralegal activities (that is, a further distortion of information flows); and covert price increases—clearly, bribing someone raises the price of the good or service sought.

Tautness means that the allotted inputs are quantitatively or qualitatively insufficient to produce the mandated outputs. Since enterprise rewards continue to be tied to output performance (despite indicator reforms) it makes sense for ministries and enterprises to assure their sources of materials supply by vertical integration. Thus, as an example, it is not unusual for machine tools enterprises to have their own coal and iron mines, steel-making facilities, and so on. This phenomenon is known as "compartmentalism" or "empire building" and will be dealt with more fully later. At this point we need note only that compartmentalization of the economy is generally wasteful, resulting in duplication and even worse shortages.

The Neglect of Demand

The process of goal formulation in the contemporary Soviet-type economy neglects the customer in general and the final consumer in particular. The planners do not intend this, nor do the executors of the planners' commands. Neglect of demand is a necessary consequence of the system. There are several reasons for this:

The system is one of vertical links and information flows. Factual information on the state of the economy together with opinions on desirable outcomes goes up, and mandatory instructions come down. Vertical information flows represent what I would call "indentured" relationships among participants in contrast to (market-type) horizontal information flows that represent "contractual" relationships. Indentured relationships are at best benevolently paternalistic; at all times they are hierarchical and authoritarian. The primary responsibility of an economic unit, whatever its position in the hierarchy, is toward its immediate superior, not to its customers. The customers' interest (in any event very imperfectly communicated to the planner and supplier) is not the one that brings a convincing reward to the supplying unit. Invariably it will be sacrificed. To remedy this situation, the reforms have made sales performance an important criterion of enterprise success, sales being presumably an indicator of "marketability" tied to user interest. However, "sales" can be carried out without delivery; at the very least, delivery can be scheduled to suit the convenience of the seller. In a system of upward enterprise responsibility and downward flow of rewards, contract enforcement tends to be very casual. There's no money in it.

Sellers' markets breed a "like it or lump it" attitude of the seller toward the buyer. This attitude is not improved by the monopolistic position of the supplier vis-a-vis his customers.

There is no mechanism in the system for customer demand to manifest itself in any allocatively meaningful way. The customer has no direct influence on prices, nor are prices in the system intended to be carriers of information to the supplier on customer wants and needs.

Marxian value theory does not analyze demand. The Soviet-type economy's pricing practice mirrors this omission.

The neglect of user needs works against economic modernization. As a chronic condition it makes little economic sense.

SELF-RELIANCE

Self-reliance has two meanings. Externally, it means concentration on domestic sources of capital formation, import substitution, and relegation of foreign trade to residual or passive status. In the contemporary Soviet economy external transactions are insulated from the domestic economy by the state's foreign trade monopoly. Foreign trade prices, in particular, are not allowed to influence the domestic price structure. Export goods are purchased from domestic suppliers by the state foreign trade corporations at domestic prices and are sold abroad at bilaterally negotiated or world market prices. Similarly, goods are purchased abroad by the corporations at bilaterally negotiated or world market prices and then sold to domestic users at domestic prices. Any profits or losses on the transactions are absorbed by the corporations and transferred to the state treasury. Internally, self-reliance means either vertical integration by industrial branches or enterprises, or horizontal (regional, territorial) integration, with the purpose of lessening the dependence of the industry or enterprise on unreliable and unpredictable outside sources of materials supply.

External Self-Reliance

The original Stalinist system's emphasis on self-reliance stemmed from the size of the country, unwillingness of foreign capitalist countries to lend a hand on any significant scale in the construction of Soviet socialism, [7] Stalin's reluctance to become involved in external transactions (seen by him as politically risky and ideologically corrupting), Soviet planners' unwillingness to have their developmental plans disrupted by imported business cycles, and a general sentiment in favor of "infant industry" protection.

Self-reliance has been reinterpreted liberally since the reforms. Soviet-type economies have become active traders not only among themselves but with market-oriented economies as well. Intensive growth requires a sustained flow of technological and scientific information, both domestic and foreign. The contemporary Soviet-type economies, highly involved as they are in external trading, implicitly admit that the past avoidance of foreign economic entanglements had been costly in terms of the benefits that could have accrued from comparative advantage. Specifically, four major steps have been taken to upgrade the status of foreign trade in the overall planning process:

The Ministry of Foreign Trade, which at one time exercised quasi-dictatorial powers over external economic transactions in behalf of the planners, has been shorn of some of its former prerogatives in favor of other ministries, branch production associations, and even enterprises. In some countries this diffusion has gone farther than in others (for example, the Soviet Union).

A new system of incentives has been worked out with the aim of stimulating exports. In some countries enterprises are allowed to retain a part of the foreign exchange earned through their exports. The attempt clearly is to build up a viable export sector, something that had been neglected under the Stalinist dispensation.

Funds have been allocated more generously to finance imports, especially imports of advanced technology from the West and Japan.

Official policy toward various forms of joint ventures has been liberalized. The liberalization has been greatest in regard to joint ventures with other Soviet-type economies, but it has also been extended, though more cautiously, to the West and Japan.

Despite these departures from the old model, some key Stalinist institutional arrangements in respect to foreign trade remain. Specifically, the insulation of the domestic from the world economy has not changed. This separation has several negative consequences for the Soviet-type economy's quest for modernization. The most obvious is the continued protection of domestic industries—that can no longer be categorized as "infant"—from foreign competition. The result is the maintenance of many relatively inefficient, high-cost enterprises. This policy is buttressed by the general principle espoused by the planners that no socialist enterprise must be allowed to die. The arrangement is cozy but wasteful and socially expensive. Another handicap is the insulation of the foreign seller from the final domestic user of the imported good. While practice varies among countries, the foreign seller normally does not meet with the final user but only with representatives of the relevant state foreign trade corporation. (The Chinese do occasionally permit representatives of the final user to sit in on the negotiations.) The reverse is also true. As a rule domestic enterprises are not put in direct contact with foreign buyers but have to deal through the trade corporation bureaucracy. The likelihood is real that the final user knows better what his needs are than does the trade corporation. Domestic producers have little incentive to explore the pattern of foreign demand so as to gear their production to foreign customers' requirements. Thus the neglect of the customer is extended to foreign markets.

A major problem arises from the absence of reliable means to compare internal and external costs. Exchange rates are multi-tiered and arbitrary; they are not of much help in domestic micro and macro planning. In fact, a good deal of trade is carried on in a rule-of-thumb, physical way without calculating relative effectiveness; if there is a shortage of particular goods, import those goods; if there is a surplus, offer them for sale abroad. All this, plus the fact that internal prices reveal neither resource scarcity relationships nor relative consumer utilities, means that there is no automatic device that would show the planners what should be imported and exported. The reformers of the 1960s devoted much of their intellectual effort to working out a methodology that could provide planners with criteria of foreign trade effectiveness. The success of this venture has been quite modest.

Internal Self-Reliance

As suggested above, this consists of a systemic propensity toward "empire building," a compartmentalization of the economy along industrial branch, enterprise, or regional lines. The reasons are taut planning (causing input shortages), bureaucratic planning (interdepartmental rivalry for inputs and rewards), priority planning (the "buffer" effect of shortages on lower-priority sectors, industries, and firms), and the system's operational tendency to discount the future (reward system linked to the fulfillment of immediate tasks, especially output targets).

Internal self-reliance, much practiced in China, has certain advantages. For the user it may obviate the uncertainties of supply inherent in his dependence on plan-designated, often distant, always harassed suppliers, thereby raising the general level of material welfare experienced by customers. It helps drum up bonuses for timely plan fulfillment. It enables the self-reliant industry or firm to branch out and produce outside the plan a variety of goods and services, which can be informally bartered or otherwise traded with benefit to all concerned.

On the other hand, compartmentalism, particularism, and localism involve costs. Information flows are hampered, when they are not altogether blocked. This has adverse effects on the diffusion of innovation and the center's attempt to assure internal consistency in planning. There is duplication and waste of scarce factors and raw materials, partly through the sacrifice of specialization and the disregard for economies of scale. The propensity of the system to generate dissimulation is strengthened. Informal lateral links and autonomous nodes of decision-making power are established in an institutional setting that is philosophically and legally hostile to them.

MOTIVATION

The nature and pattern of incentives are very important in determining the quantitative and qualitative performance of an economy. The contemporary Soviet-type economy relies primarily on differentiated, competitive, material incentives directed at individuals. The stress is on rewards rather than punishments. This system is supplemented by differentiated, competitive, moral, and material incentives directed at groups. Most of these emerge from mass emulation drives ("socialist competition"). Compared with the original Stalinist model, current incentives are less differentiated, less competitive, and based more on "value" indicators. They are generally more positive, although disincentives in the form of fines and incarceration are still in evidence.

One of the issues that any modernizing economy must grapple with is how to give individual workers and managers a sense of participation in a broader common purpose, how to reconcile the interests of individuals and individual economic units with the broader interests of the collectivity—the public good, as articulated by the state. Philosophically, in capitalist societies this problem has been relegated for solution to the competitive market, supplemented in more recent times by income redistribution and other governmental corrective actions. The problem is posed acutely in socialist societies that are explicitly committed to the attainment of harmony between collective and individual interests. In such societies the primitive answer to the problem has been socialization of the means of production. It is clear, however, to all but the more obtuse doctrinaires, that socialization—while not without important social, political, and economic effects—does not by itself provide an answer to the alienation of the micro unit from the collective purpose. Given the tendency of socialized property to be tightly controlled by the monoparty center, the alienation problem looms larger rather than disappearing. One interesting attempt at a solution has been made by the Yugoslavs. It has taken the form of institutionalized worker participation in the management of enterprises through the agency of elected workers' councils and the association of enterprises in the conduct of the national economy by means of various linkages to local commune authorities, and the devolution by the center to enterprise managements of broad operational property rights in the means of production. This approach has been rejected by the Soviet-type economy as an aberration and a serious misreading of the Marxist message. For a time—during and for a few years after the Cultural Revolution—China experimented with its own version of participation: the enterprise revolutionary committees and other three-way combinations of workers, managers, and technicians (or alternatively, the young, the old, and the middle-aged), backed by the right to put up big character posters.

The contemporary Soviet-type economy attempts to reconcile diverse worker, manager, and state interests through a theoretically sophisticated system of profit sharing rather than through copartnership institutionalized in workers' councils or revolutionary committees. This is an indirect way of tackling the participation problem, via the system of rewards, rather than directly through association of workers in enterprise management and association of enterprises in national planning.

Directorial Principle

The contemporary Soviet-type economy, like its Stalinist prototype, employs the directorial principle of enterprise management, an offshoot of the broader principle of democratic centralism. The principle states that since the manager represents the important grassroots link in the highly structured, hierarchical, administrative chain of command, he is the boss of the enterprise and the workers must obey him, and he is personally responsible to his superiors (not to his workers) for the fulfillment of the plan and the proper management of the assets of the firm, this fulfillment and management being expressed through the system of economic accountability (khozraschet). Hence, to be enterprise manager confers power within the firm and status within the system. As in the old manorial system these benefits are contingent on the manager's carrying out a host of duties, obligations, and responsibilities toward his hierarchical betters. Because of this duality of power and personal responsibility in a complex bureaucracy and within the framework of taut plans, the manager's job is as difficult and tense as that of any executive of a Western business corporation; probably more so. The average tenure of office of managers in the system tends to be brief. It is not just that enterprise management is a step on the long ladder of administrative preferment and that managers naturally want to climb up the ladder. As has already been suggested, the system forces the managers into almost daily conflict with the law, and one way of avoiding the day of reckoning is to keep on moving, if not up, then laterally along the managerial rung.

The manager's powers are limited, of course, in various ways. The most obvious limitation is that his power is a power to execute within the enterprise orders received from above. It is not the right to make allocative decisions in the influential sense of choosing what to produce, how, for whom, and at what price to sell the output in response to horizontal, freely contracted relations with customers. Managerial power in the Soviet-type economy is the power of an army sergeant. Given this basic limitation on managerial discretion it would make little sense to have workers share in that power through some formal organizational procedure. The workers clearly perceive that the manager is only an executor of orders, just as they are, but on a somewhat more elevated plane. In some countries of the Soviet-type system provisions exist for worker consultative committees, but they are sickly organizations. Further encroachment on managerial prerogatives is made by party organs. The precise relationship of the party to management varies over time, but the principle that the party has the right to intervene in managerial affairs is well established and commonly indulged in. Trade unions in the system are no longer just transmission belts for the center's orders about labor discipline. They do participate with management in decisions on bonus distribution to workers and play an important role in the administration of the firm's welfare funds. The unions act as spokesmen for the workers on matters of industrial safety. In all these respects they restrict the power of the enterprise director.

It is probably true that the technological and administrative imperatives of modern management call for something like the directorial principle in any economic system. Even the Yugoslav experiment suggests that it is difficult to run a factory by democratic vote and broad debate. The functions, prerogatives, and responsibilities of the manager in the Soviet-type economy are microcosms of the whole system and make sense within such an arrangement.

The main problem is tutelage: the enterprise director's bonded relationship to higher authority. Except indirectly and precariously, through the kind of information he sends upward and what he can get away with, the enterprise director is no more a dominant participant in the system than are workers. Even in the execution of planners' commands within the enterprise, the director is hemmed in by many formal and informal indicators communicated to him by a multitude of supervisory agencies. I think this has a profoundly negative effect on the manager's initiative. It makes him risk averse. Like the rest of the bureaucracy, he takes on the uninspiringly grey hue of routine.[8]

A second problem is that despite the injunction that the enterprise manager is personally responsible for his actions within the plan, personal responsibility in a huge and complex administrative organization is extremely difficult to pinpoint. It is in the nature of bureaucracies to be faceless and dissolve the locus of responsibility in a sea of bureaus, committees, and subcommittees. The directorial principle becomes in everyday practice the scapegoat principle. When things go really wrong, an enterprise manager will be selected for public chastisement, pour encourager les autres.

There is also the possibility, amply borne out by history, of a contradiction arising between the interests of enterprise managements (in terms of the success indicators communicated to them by the planners) and the interests of the rank-and-file workers. Such incompatibilities are, of course, also present in capitalist corporations and, in a seeming paradox, even in a worker-managed Yugoslav firm. The key element is the workers' capacity to assert their interest in an organized fashion, through labor unions, for example. This element is absent in the Soviet-type economy. While trade unions have acquired wider powers since the death of Stalin, they remain creatures of the state, vested with the task of safeguarding the state interest. They have very little say in the determination of tariff wages and are not permitted to strike. Unless the interests of workers and managements can be organically linked, the directorial principle, with its stress on the manager's upward responsibility, makes intrafirm labor conflict (or at least repressed tension) almost certain.

The Bonus

The manager's total income is made up of four ingredients: basic (or tariff) salary, bonus, social wage (social security income), and fringe benefits ("perks" and other administered privileges). I shall concentrate here on the bonus component of managerial income because it represents a theoretically interesting attempt to establish an organic link between planners' and enterprise interests.

A couple of brief remarks on basic (tariff) salary: Salary schedules for managerial personnel are prepared at a high planning level and usually indicate ranges for various types of enterprises within different industries. The level of salary will reflect the position of the sector, industry, and enterprise on the planners' scale of preferences. Thus, managers of textile enterprises will normally receive lower basic salaries than managers of steel works. Nove notes that in the Soviet Union the differentials between tariff wages paid to higher-skilled workers and basic salaries of managers are nowadays probably too narrow from the standpoint of incentives. [9]

The manager in the contemporary Soviet-type economy is a bonus maximizer. If he plays his cards right, he can substantially raise his basic salary and also establish a good record for himself in the eyes of his superiors. The bonus is usually tied to target fulfillment rather than overfulfillment. This is intended to encourage managers to transmit to the planners fairly truthful information at the stage of plan preparation and to cease the practice of gunning for a "soft" plan by understating capacity and overstating needs. The bonus may take the form of more or less regular additions to basic salaries, special payment for specific accomplishments, or a lump sum paid at the end of the year for overall performance under the plan. The managerial bonus is paid exclusively out of an enterprise bonus fund (or material incentive fund) formed from the portion of profits retained by the enterprise. Although there exist, as we shall see, centrally determined regulations regarding payments into and out of the bonus fund, managerial discretion over bonus payments is greater than over basic salaries. Within the parameters set by the planners for bonus distribution, the manager can adapt his behavior in a variety of ways designed to maximize his bonus without jeopardizing the future flow of premia.

Let us now see how the system works, what its strengths and its weaknesses are. The manager receives from superior agencies plan norms (targets, indicators) for current and future production (investment). These norms are expressed in physical and financial (value) terms. To the manager the centrally formulated norms are indicators of his success at fulfilling the planners' instructions. Because of the large number of indicators and their imperfect fit (internal consistency), some indicators are more important to the planners—and hence to the manager—than others. The first managerial problem, therefore, is to find out which indicators are important and which are less important; which must be carried out to the full, and which can be trimmed without the sky falling. The manager's career and his material welfare are bound up with 100 percent fulfillment of the key indicators. Since the reform of the Stalinist model, financial indicators have assumed comparatively more importance, and among these the norms of profit, profitability, and sales are of particular significance to the planners' perception of enterprise success. Profits and profitability rates are supposedly indicators of efficiency and sales are said to show marketability, qualities that had been deficient under the old system. Sheer bulk of production has not been abandoned. Sales, profitabilities, and profits count only on condition that the targets for output volume and assortment have been carried out. Finally, increases in labor productivity have been given much prominence since the reforms. To sum up: in the contemporary Soviet-type economy the major managerial success indicators are profits, profitability, sales, output volume, assortment, and labor productivity.[10]

Physical Norms

The centrally formulated norms of managerial performance are both physical and financial. The physical norms are expressed in weights, linear and other measures, and in various technical coefficients (production functions). As has just been noted, they retain their importance within the plan despite the upgrading of value indicators. The first problem with physical norms is that they are unidimensional, that is, they indicate only one dimension of performance. Consequently they readily lend themselves to distortion: a plan for the manufacture of sheet glass expressed in square meters tends to result in the production of very thin glass; expressed in weight, it produces only very thick glass—unless, that is, the first indicator is backed by another physical norm (for example, specification of assortment), in which case a new distortion will occur (for example, lowering of quality), necessitating the mobilization of an endless succession of indicators. By the time the planners are through straightening out managerial perversity, there are too many physical indicators. These are often incompatible and, therefore, cannot all be carried out; they are sure to conflict in several places with corresponding value indicators. Hence they must be ranked again; in which case the managers will read the planners' ranking anew and adapt their behavior accordingly. In the meantime information costs within the system rise. The managers will try to prevent the planners from discovering their twisting of the planners' intent; the planners will multiply monitoring authorities to uncover disobedient behavior by managers; erroneous decisions will be made based on erroneous information from the field; and numerous ad hoc adjustments in the course of plan execution will have to be made, leading to new feats of behavioral calisthenics on the part of managers.

The second problem with physical planning techniques (other than linear programming) is that by themselves they will not give allocative optimality readings. Input-output tables and material balances can be used to arrive at internal consistency of physical decisions, but not at static allocative efficiency. Reliance on physical indicators will not provide an impulse for cost minimization. In other words, in a system dominated by physical planning norms, optimality can be arrived at only by chance. More typically, there will be a wasteful use of resources.

It was the realization that this kind of blindman's buff could not be allowed to go on indefinitely that in the 1960s sparked interest not only in linear programming techniques, but in what were then seen as multidimensional, "synthetic" value indicators. Profits, profitability, sales, and so on, it was argued, sum up a large number of behavioral dimensions. They can be used to help calculate allocative optimality, and they are less costly than the administration of physical norms.

Financial ("Value") Norms

"While there may be a million laws, the law of value is the most important," says the Chinese economist Sun Yehfang, who spent seven years in jail for expressing similar views back in the early 1960s.[11] Unfortunately "value" in the contemporary Soviet-type economy, and the way the "law of value" operates, will not give the planners helpful suggestions on allocative optimality.

In the broadest sense allocative optimality means minimization of waste: getting the most output from the least expenditure of the available scarce resources, that is, output should be produced with the combination of inputs that is least burdensome to society, and every input should be used where it gives the biggest possible output. The mix of consumer goods and services should match exactly what consumers really want, and the goods exported should be those that earn the most foreign exchange for a given amount of domestic resources used in producing the export goods.[12]

Information on whether or not allocative optimality is being approached is provided by opportunity cost prices. Such prices reflect the usefulness of goods to the user and the relative real costs of producing the goods. With few exceptions prices in the contemporary Soviet-type economy are not opportunity cost prices. They do not indicate utility to the user or relative real production costs— they do not even reflect the preferences of the planners accurately. There are at least two reasons why this is so:

Marxist value theory takes no account of demand. In the contemporary Soviet-type economy an attempt is made to factor demand into prices, but the exercise is theoretically deficient and quite subsidiary in practice. Industrial wholesale prices, which are the basis of state retail prices in the contemporary Soviet-type economy, are average branch cost-plus prices adjusted to exclude high-cost (marginal) producers and take account of planned increases in labor productivity; and they are weighted by the output levels of the various enterprises in the branch. The "plus" is represented by profit margins that include a fairly arbitrary capital charge (or "interest") on the average annual value of the enterprise's undepreciated total capital. This charge is really an extra tax on profits, not in any way an indicator of the opportunity cost of the factor capital. [13]

Prices as guides to allocative optimality require ongoing adjustments in response to continuous changes in the underlying demand and supply-cost conditions. In the Soviet-type economy such price adjustments are infrequent and, when made, are made with a lag for three reasons: First, price adjustments are carried out manually by planners at a high level of the administrative hierarchy. Information on changes in demand (especially consumer demand) and cost conditions are communicated to the price adjusters administratively by many subordinate agencies. This takes time, so there will be a lag. Second, the job of monitoring several million individual prices is big and burdensome; some changes in underlying conditions will not be spotted at all, others will be misread. Third, the system has an inbuilt preference for price stability. Stability of the consumer price level is, it will be recalled, one of the objectives of the system. (Periodic startling, usually upward, adjustments in retail prices that brutally tear away the consumers' money illusion have been known to result in public riots and defenestration of party officials by outraged citizens.) General stability of prices (especially wholesale prices and farm procurement prices) is seen as desirable for purposes of planning at both the level of the central planning board and that of the individual enterprise, especially for farming enterprise. Hence prices in the system depart significantly from scarcity and demand;[14] they are chronically in disequilibrium. Besides, even after the reforms, the system's prices are at best secondary information carriers. Fulfillment of key physical indicators remains the sine qua non for management's being awarded bonuses for profit, profitability, and sales performance.

Because prices in the contemporary Soviet-type economy are not efficiency prices, the profits based on those prices and profitability rates tell nothing about allocative optimality. They remain, as before, simple accounting devices. To be "synthetic" indicators of allocative optimality, prices must provide information on relative costs of competing alternative courses of action; on substitution possibilities at the margin of decisions. Sticky average branch cost-plus prices do not do this and the profits that emerge from the constellation of such prices are unidimensional, not unlike the physical indicators upon which they were supposed to be an improvement. "There is no rational link in the Soviet system between prices and profits and the needs of society," not even of societal needs as perceived by the planners. [15] With few exceptions, differences in profitability are not indicative of planners', producers', or consumers' micro preferences. [16]

Enterprise Bonus Fund

An important measure intended to reconcile the interests of the state with those of enterprises and enterprise managers has been the enterprise bonus fund (or material incentives fund) formed out of that portion of enterprise profits not taken away by the center. [17] This mechanism appears also to be under consideration in post-Mao China. The enterprise stimulation funds (there are three of them: a bonus fund, a production development fund, and a fund for social-cultural projects) represent a conservative compromise on the matter of decentralization. The enterprise is given some discretionary powers, but these are circumscribed by detailed, centrally promulgated rules and regulations and (with the exception of the bonus fund) are confined to extra plan activities and contingent on the availability of resources outside the plan—a condition that does not often materialize in the setting of taut planning and endemic resource shortages.

The operation of the bonus fund, especially as regards payments into the fund, has been well described by Rosenberg. [18] The procedure is roughly as follows:

At the outset of a five-year plan, enterprise managements are given an array of production, sales, productivity, profits, and other targets that the planners expect to be fulfilled during the five-year period, with breakdowns for each year. This plan is accompanied by a ruble figure known as the Plan Fulfillment Bonus (PFB) that represents not the actual amount of bonus that will accrue to the enterprise management upon plan fulfillment, but rather a base figure from which the actual bonus is to be calculated after the enterprise's annual performance is known and two sets of adjustments are made in the PFB.

At the end of the year, when performance for the year is known, the PFB is adjusted in a first round by applying to it coefficients based on three plan indicators: output value, gross profit, and labor productivity. The resulting figure is known as the Plan Fulfillment Bonus (provisional) or PFB_p. The PFB_p may be larger, smaller, or the same as the PFB, depending on the importance that the planners attach to plan fulfillment, overfulfillment, or underfulfillment. Normally PFB_p will be smaller than PFB if the plan is underfulfilled, even if only by a small percentage (this is in line with the sharp discontinuities in goals referred to earlier). Nowadays overfulfillment of the three targets will not normally be rewarded by higher bonuses in order to discourage managers from proposing artificially low targets that can be easily exceeded.

A second set of adjustments is then made. The PFB_p figure is multiplied by two additional coefficients based on plan targets for sales revenue and net profits. The first is believed to represent marketability of the product, the second enterprise efficiency (especially as regards reduction of material intensity). The resulting figure is known as the Plan Fulfillment Bonus (Final), or PFB_f. The PFB_f represents the final amounts of monies authorized for distribution to managerial and technical personnel and—to a lesser extent—to workers. Payments out of the PBF_f are governed by centrally formulated, complex, and varied rules. Normally disbursements are made quarterly. The actual intraenterprise bonus distribution takes the form of additions to the basic (tariff) wages and salaries, special payments for particular achievements, or year-end premia linked to overall annual performance under the plan.

Theoretically the system appears to achieve its main purpose, namely to make the overall performance of the enterprise a matter of common concern to managers and workers, without Yugoslav-type councils and other formal copartnership organizations. The system also enables the center to align enterprise and social interests (the latter as perceived by the planners) by the simple expedient of adjusting the various coefficients applied to the base bonus figure (PFB). Since the PFB is announced and fixed in advance for each of the five years, as are also the key performance indicators, the system would seem to discourage managers from holding down production because of the fear that performance indicators will be raised in subsequent years if the enterprise reveals its full production potential (the "ratchet" principle).

By and large, practice so far has unfortunately not borne out the expectations of theory. Changes in plan indicators continue to be made during the planning year in response to sudden changes in "objective" circumstances or because of shifts in the leaders' perceptions. Since profit in the system is not a correct indicator of social welfare, enterprise managers concentrate on profit to the extent that it affects their personal pocketbooks. The welfare of the managerial pocket can be enhanced by sacrificing other lower-priority plan indicators, usually product quality and assortment. Sometimes a quick profit can be turned by using expensive, high-grade materials when cheaper and lower-grade inputs would have done as well or better. In other words, the problem of material intensity has not been solved. Because managements have relatively wide powers in the matter of the precise modalities of sharing out PFB_f monies within the firm, all kinds of bonus distribution distortions have been reported. Sometimes PFB_f funds are handed out equally; at other times highly skilled workers receive inordinately high bonuses because managements are anxious to retain them in a general setting of tight labor supply. The positive effects of the planners' ability to manipulate the coefficients in response to changed circumstances are countered by managerial apprehension that should the plan be even slightly overfulfilled, the coefficients (if not the base PFB figure or plan indicators) will be adjusted by the planners, thus effectively reducing the PFB_f. Because of persistent sharp goal discontinuities, even a slight underfulfillment of plan targets entails significant reductions in total managerial salaries. So it is still the better part of wisdom for managers to understate their production capacities and put reserves out of the planners' sight. Rosenberg notes an interesting variant on the old storming technique.[19] Since managerial bonuses are as a rule paid quarterly on the basis of adjusted annual coefficients, managers will tend to concentrate production on the first three quarters to earn high bonuses and then reduce effort in the fourth quarter so as to bring down annual performance to levels that are safe in light of the planners' continued propensity to employ the ratchet principle. Before the reform, work was slack in the first three quarters and accelerated in the last quarter. Thus, the annual production cycle instead of being eliminated has merely been recycled. The timing of its rhythm has been altered; that is all.

The intent to create a commonality of interests between planners, managers, and workers through the incentive mechanism is further diluted by the relatively small part that enterprise profits play in production worker bonuses. The bulk of such bonuses still comes from the wages fund.

I think it would not be incorrect to conclude that in the Soviet-type economy the relationship of the three major actors—planners, managers, and workers—remains antagonistic.

INNOVATION

Science and technological innovation are held high in the estimation of those in charge of the contemporary Soviet-type economy.

A career in science or engineering is one of the surer means of upward social mobility and improved material welfare for the individual. As early as 1957 the Soviet Union was graduating 80,000 engineers a year to America's 30,000, and the ratio has been bettered by the Soviets since. Investment in science and technology in all contemporary Soviet-type economies is heavy, and there have been some spectacular achievements.[20] A persistent complaint, however, is that the results are not commensurate with the effort expended: that the rate of innovation is too low, that the implementation of inventions is too slow, and that the gap between the scientific and technological accomplishments of Soviet-type and market-oriented Western economies is growing.

I think lagging technology—except in the highest-priority areas, such as military hardware—is inherent in the Soviet-type system of social organization. Most of the reasons have already been touched upon, but it will do no harm to review them briefly again.

Centralization

Innovation in the Soviet-type economy, like most other things, is centrally inspired, planned, directed, and implemented. It flows from the top down in the form of specific instructions as to particular areas of exploratory need. Unplanned, spontaneous innovation in the lower reaches of the organizational pyramid, while rhetorically encouraged and rewarded with all sorts of prizes and moral commendations, has little chance of making its way sufficiently high up the bureaucratic hierarchy to be seriously considered, embodied in the overall plan, and implemented.

In addition to the tendency of a highly centralized system to deal lightly with final user needs, there are difficulties flowing from the absence of effective lateral information channels in the economy. Suppose the central planners (in the guise of, for example, a high-level State Committee on Science and Technology) wish to introduce a particular piece of advanced hardware. Instructions to develop such equipment are sent to research institutes and design bureaus; the order to produce it is given to a particular enterprise; production of complementary equipment, components, and software is assigned to someone else. Because these various agents lack lateral links, the conception, design, and production of the new equipment, which in the nature of things should be highly coordinated, is disjointed and subject to the payoff pulls of several diverse microunit success indicators.[21]

Also, given the sharp discontinuities in the ranking of planners' goals, what are considered by the planners to be lower-priority items going into the new piece of equipment (or items technically essential to the operation of the equipment) will often be late in coming, or of inferior quality, or the wrong assortment, thus delaying and impairing the efficient operation of the new device.

Short Time Horizons

The main thrust of the contemporary Soviet-type economy is toward the accomplishment of short-run, practical, applied, tangible tasks. We have had occasion to note that one of the unresolved contradictions between planners and enterprise managers is that while the planners look toward the future, the managers are rewarded for what they do in the present with slight reference to the longer run, that is, the planners' "evaluative time horizons" are shorter than the planners' aspirations. The incentive mechanism is tied up with immediate results and the system is obsessed with day-to-day output. Innovation means retooling; retooling tends to have negative effects on profit and output rates in the present; loss of output in the present means loss of bonuses at the end of the quarter or year.

To remedy this, special enterprise production development funds were set up and design organizations were organizationally separated from the production command structure of enterprises, all of which did not improve matters a great deal. The problem is not so much to come up with a new idea as to implement the idea coherently, without throwing other plan indicators (especially the bonus-related ones) out of kilter. In fact, the separation of production management from design and innovation departments seems to have made things worse. Managements complained that designers kept coming up with "impractical" ideas—impractical in the way plan norms operated for enterprises. The designers, managers argued, had no accounting and production responsibilities. The success indicators applicable to them were not the same as those applying to the enterprise; indeed, they were often at odds. Frequently, innovators were (and are) rewarded for the number of innovations they came up with, whatever the temporary effects on enterprise output, sales, profits, and other rewarding current indicators. On the other hand, managers strived to maximize (or at least "satisfize") their bonuses under the operative payoff formulae.

So recourse was had to two other expedients: The first is the amalgamation of enterprises into larger firms (production associations), each equipped with research (including market research) and design organizations, and experimental production, testing, and serial production facilities, and endowed with decision-making powers superior to those of its formerly independent enterprise components. These combines were large enough to venture into technical forecasting and spread the costs of research and development ment over a large enough volume of product. Assuming no intra-combine obstacles to information transfer, these new organizational units seem to be theoretically capable of overcoming the problems caused by the absence in the system of lateral interenterprise links. The second major expedient consists in the establishment of large research and development (R&D) corporations that possess an array of forecasting, research, design, prototype production, and testing facilities, all functioning under an integrated system of operational managerial payoff formulae. The fully developed model is submitted to the planners for possible insertion into the national economic plan. The Soviet aircraft industry has used this general expedient with comparatively positive results. [22]

Conservatism

The system, as we have seen, is noted for risk avoidance, which is the antithesis of innovation. Risk aversion has come to be more pronounced as the bureaucratic apparatus has aged and become increasingly removed from its original revolutionary impetus. The comparative safety of routine is emerging as a respectable objective of the system despite reforms intended to revitalize the economy.

Enterprise Immortality

Like old soldiers, socialist enterprises never die; nor do they go bankrupt. In these circumstances the urge to innovate, so as to get an edge on one's competitor or simply survive, is not among the more compelling drives experienced by managers.

Administrative Barriers

There exist in the system bureaucratic barriers to the diffusion of technology. Some of these arise from the complexity of the administrative network and its sluggishness. Some are due to the already discussed propensity of ministries and enterprises to build for themselves vertically integrated empires as insurance against supply shortages. Information of all kinds, including information about inventions and innovations, tends to become sealed within the walls of the branch bureaucracy, until such time as superior authority stumbles upon it and orders the information diffused.

Price Inflexibility and Customer Neglect

Since prices in the system are, by and large, inflexible and fail to reflect user wants (in fact are not intended to act as users' messages to producers), there is little opportunity for customers to show their preferences for superior product design and better quality by bidding up the price of the product. The system fails to associate the user in the drive for scientific and technological innovation.

The combination of these several causalities has given rise to a good deal of illusory innovation intended by managers to take advantage of a given constellation of success indicators. For example, although most prices are set by the planners, prices of certain goods produced for the first time or otherwise "new" can be priced temporarily by the enterprise in conjunction with its supervisory ministry. If profit is a rewarding indicator, it will pay to innovate by, for example, changing the shape of the bottle or putting on a new label, pricing the "new" product high compared with the old one (now discontinued), and cashing in the economic profits until such time as the upper hierarchies get around to rolling back the inflated prices.

PLANNING

Central planning in the contemporary Soviet-type economy has two main components: physical and financial (or "value"). From the mid-1960s, when the Stalinist system was reformed, both components have been refined and—with the upgrading of value planning—have come to share, if not an equal status, at least a less unequal one. The refinement concerned the theories, underlying physical and financial planning as well as the specific tools used. Since that time an outpouring of theoretical speculation in both the Soviet Union and Eastern Europe has taken place. Much progress has been made in elaborating, at an abstract level, more effective techniques in planning the allocation of resources. Because the translation of theoretical models into economic policy is a political-bureaucratic matter, the introduction of new concepts and tools of planning into the economy has been considerably more sluggish and cautious than intellectual speculation. It can, in fact, be argued that the slow pace of institutional reform and the conservatism with which it is infused have created new problems on top of the old. The new problems are due in large measure to the incompatibility of the novel concepts and planning tools with those surviving from the days of the ancien regime. [23]

Physical Planning

This component consists in the setting by the planners of current production and investment targets in tons, meters, liquid measures, technical coefficients, number of units, and so on, with specification of assortment, and a corresponding determination by the planners of input norms in physical and technical terms with specification of assortment.

To date, two related kinds of tools have been used for this purpose in the contemporary Soviet-type economy. The most common has been the so-called material balance technique, which is essentially a series of partial and disaggregated input-output tables applied to specific industries and commodities. The major characteristics of this technique are as follows:

The balances do not cover all the goods produced and used by the economy: some goods are not covered at all, while others may be included in a very aggregated way in those balances that are calculated. Moreover, for reasons endemic to the system, not all the production of a commodity for which a balance is constructed is always included in the balance. In short, material balances are internally incomplete and the system of balances is not comprehensive.

The individual commodity balances are not well integrated with one another, nor is the network of commodity balances properly reconciled with other balances of the national economy (for example, labor, financial balances).

Because of the three major gaps (in commodities covered by material balances, between individual commodity balances, and between the commodity balances network and other balances of the economy), it is well-nigh impossible to establish intercommodity and intersector consistency of resource supply and distribution. Consistency requires that any change in the output of one commodity be accompanied by changes in the output of all products directly (first-order relationship) or indirectly (second-, third-, fourth-, . . . order relationships) entering as inputs into the production of that commodity. Because of the absence of the necessary linkages in Soviet-type physical planning, the balancing process will concentrate primarily on reconciling the supply and distribution of single commodities, rather than on reconciling different commodity balances. When an attempt is made at interbalance reconciliation, such an attempt will normally be limited to only those balances that are linked by first-order relationships. Changes in second-, third-, and fourth-order relationships are made only where such changes are highly visible. [24] More usually, inconsistencies between planned inputs and outputs are allowed to work themselves out through bottlenecks, shortages, and other minor and major annoyances that, as a rule, are either shifted to the lower-priority "buffer" sectors of the economy (for example, consumer goods), or resolved in grey and black markets.

The balances established for individual "commodities" are really balances for broad classifications of commodities, the components of each class being linked by technical conversion factors (for example, horsepower, nutrient component of chemical fertilizers, BTU, and so on). Thus, the major "commodity" classifications include such items as ferrous metals, chemicals, cement, meat, fats, and fabrics.

The major reason why the problems associated with the material balances technique have not been ironed out—in fact, why the material balances technique has been adopted in the first place—is that even in a simple economy the task of physically balancing the supplies and demands of commodities and other factors is formidable. In the Soviet Union, even with the help of sophisticated computer hardware, the problem of arriving at internal consistency of physical planning decisions remains as elusive as ever. Except in the most favored industries, the contemporary Soviet-type economy is marked by quasi-permanent disequilibria between supply and demand: shortages of wanted goods and surpluses of unwanted ones. In short, the system lacks internal consistency.

A more advanced tool of physical planning is the comprehensive input-output table. All contemporary Soviet-type economies have experimented with it in increasingly elaborate ways. It has been an educational process of potentially far-reaching consequences for central planning. Experiments with input-output tables have demonstrated that political authorities should confine themselves to expressing the final demand desired by them "in the national interest," such as consumption and investment, but without specific output and input goals. Instead of concerning themselves with specific growth rates of the producer goods sector as against the consumer goods sector (or "heavy" versus "light" industry), the political bosses of the planners should define the relative claims on final output of investment and consumption. "The proper procedure is to start here, and then to work through the input-output table to implications for the growth of the textile industry versus the growth of the rubber industry, rather than trying to specify industrialization strategies in terms of gross output directly."[25]

The input-output technique of physical planning, if widely adopted, would increase the probability of arriving at internal consistency of allocative decisions within the contemporary Soviet-type economy, but it would not assure the optimality of such decisions.

The reason is that the input-output technique is limited to balancing supplies with final and intermediate demands, but it does not take into account the substitutability of inputs.

However, a mathematical-geometrical technique for optimizing allocative decisions in the context of a physically planned economy exists, even though its application on an economywide scale raises some difficult problems. The technique known as linear programming was invented in the Soviet Union by a mathematician, L. V. Kantorovich. Linear programming is a potentially powerful means of reducing waste motion in centrally planned economies and allocating resources in ways that maximize the attainment of plan-determined goals. The technique embraces all the key elements of Western value theory: opportunity cost, scarcity, the idea of value as an indicator of scarcity relative to the objectives set, and so on. Linear programming is now intellectually accepted in all Soviet-type societies and included in many university economics curricula. It is frequently resorted to by firms in the West to help them solve specific business planning problems. Its use in the Soviet Union for purposes of national planning is inhibited less by the complexity involved in extending the technique to the whole economy than by its theoretical-ideological implications for the surplus labor theory of value.

Economic Fluctuations

Spokesmen for central administrative planning argue that centrally planned economies are superior to market ones because, among the various things they do better, they get rid of the business cycle. With the exception of Jevons' sunspots theory,* explanations of cyclical fluctuations have centered on causes apparently inherent in the institutions of the market economy. Hence, it is said, the business cycle is a capitalist phenomenon, absent from both pre-capitalist systems and contemporary socialist centrally planned economies. In Soviet-type economic literature this contention is expressed in the "Law of Planned, Proportional Development of the National Economy." The law says that once all property in the means of production is socialized and the anarchy of the market

---

*An explanation of business cycles advanced by the British economist William Stanley Jevons (1835-1882) according to which the periodic appearance of spots on the sun affects crop growth and, therefore, overall business activity on earth.

replaced by conscious central allocation, economic fluctuations are banished and the economy develops smoothly, harmoniously, and evenly. That it does not develop harmoniously and evenly is, I think, clear from the argument made earlier regarding the sharp discontinuities in the ranking of planners' priorities and the deliberate neglect of certain sectors (for example, agriculture, consumer services) in the process of growth. It can further be argued that the contemporary Soviet-type economy, like its Stalinist predecessor, is subject to periodic fluctuations, reminiscent of the capitalist business cycle. However, it manifests itself in somewhat different forms, and is due to rather different causes.

In conventional terms, economic fluctuations refer to periodic swings in output, employment, and the general level of prices (inflation, deflation). These are thought to be socially undesirable because they increase the uncertainty inherent in the economic decision-making process, spontaneously redistribute income and the material well-being of different social classes, and generally undermine the legitimacy of the system (that is, the willingness of the system's participants to accept the status quo).

Fluctuations in output, employment, and the general level of prices are definitionally ruled out in the contemporary Soviet-type economy. Taut planning (especially strained output targets and the ratchet principle) makes for constantly rising reported output. Administrative control over prices prevents swings in the wholesale and consumer price indexes, except those that are from time to time sanctioned by the price fixers. The mobilization of labor to carry out the strained output targets, combined with the principle of life-long employment, keep employment at or near the full level. It can be said, therefore, that Soviet-type economies do not exhibit <u>overt</u> overproduction/underconsumption crises, inflation/deflation, or structural unemployment. Like individual decision-making rights, all three have been suppressed by the command institutions of the economy. It does not follow that they have ceased to exist.

Production, employment, and price fluctuations express themselves in the contemporary Soviet-type economy in suppressed (or covert) form. While gross output targets rise and are achieved year in year out, some of the output is unusable (that is, does not economically exist) because of mismatch with demand, or because of quality or assortment violations, or for a variety of other system-related reasons. There is also a considerable loss factor in output—which is not revealed in the statistics—due to inadequate storage and transport, and to theft en route from producer to user. This too fluctuates over time. As planners crack down to correct the problem, it reappears with more or less severity in other forms. There are, therefore, in contemporary Soviet-type economies <u>covert</u> output fluctuations not revealed by the official statistical series. One way of quantifying the intensity of such cycles would be by measuring the fluctuations in the product reject rate and the rising and falling frustrations of users with the goods they purchase. Clearly this would not be an easy assignment. Similarly, while overt structural unemployment is generally absent, suppressed unemployment (underemployment) is rampant in all contemporary Soviet-type economies—side by side, it should be noted, with often severe labor shortages. This underemployment fluctuates over time, depending on the brutality with which the ratchet is applied, the degree of instability of output and input norms, and other institutional factors. The contemporary Soviet-type economy also exhibits fluctuations in the underemployment of capital and materials (fluctuations in the hedge factor). The spectacle of unfinished, often unfinishable, factories and idle or semi-idle machinery is common. Depending on the precise constellation of institutional arrangements, the spectacle is more or less common. While wholesale and retail price indices (when they are published) are known for their stability over time, suppressed inflation is widespread; it is practically a component part of the system. Indeed, much of the work of the contemporary Soviet-type economy is explainable only in terms of black market transactions, mutual back scratching, and under-the-counter payments, which—like defective output, and underemployment—rise and fall in cyclical fashion.

The undesirable social consequences of business cycles (increased uncertainty of the decision-making process, redistribution of income, undermining of legitimacy) apply to contemporary Soviet-type economies as much as they do to market-oriented systems. The major difference lies in the covertness of the phenomenon and the difficulty of quantifying it in a setting of still rather miserly and sometimes inaccurate official data.

The important point to be made is that economic fluctuations in centrally planned economies of the Soviet type are endogenous to the administrative command system, rather than caused by some outside influences. More specifically, they originate in defective information flows and incentive structures.[26]

CONCLUSION

The death of Stalin provided the new Soviet leaders with an opportunity to address themselves to the urgent structural problems of the economy. The need to modernize the system was generally acknowledged. Over time it became clear that economic modernization was understood in the narrow sense of raising factor productivity, stimulating the pace of innovation, augmenting capital endowment per worker, and raising the standards of education, research, science, and technology. When it came to the subjective attributes of economic modernization—the human side of it, summed up in the need to grant individual consumers, workers, and enterprise managements broad rights to make allocative choices—the reformers drew back in horror. Administrative decentralization took the place of proposed economic decentralization; the vertical structure of information flows, administrative coordination, and the center's detailed regulation of the incentive system were not significantly altered and such "economic" and "synthetic" indicators as were introduced in no way synthesized the pattern of opportunity costs in the system. The partial reforms characterized by the uneasy coexistence of administrative-physical and accounting-financial instruments of control distorted the behavior of consumers, workers, and managers in novel ways. In short, Soviet reforms suggest that the Soviet political-economic establishment is organically incapable of surrendering meaningful decision-making powers to anyone. The retention of the monopoly of allocative power at the center remains a basic principle of Soviet conduct to this day. Plus ça change, plus c'est la même chose.

NOTES

1. Robert W. Campbell, The Soviet-Type Economies: Performance and Evolution (Boston: Houghton Mifflin, 1974), p. 22; David Granick, "An Organizational Model of Soviet Industrial Planning," Journal of Political Economy 67, no. 2 (April 1959): 109-30; Alan A. Brown and Egon Neuberger, eds., International Trade and Central Planning: An Analysis of Economic Interaction (Berkeley and Los Angeles: University of California Press, 1968), pp. 405-14; J. Wilczynski, The Economics of Socialism (Chicago: Aldine, 1970), pp. 23-24.

2. For reasons that will become clear later, the reports on past output performance are probably well below enterprise potential.

3. Campbell, op. cit., p. 47. To Lenin, democracy was not an arithmetic concept (majority rule), but a political one: a question of who is more in tune with historical progress, that is, the vanguard (communist) party, however small it may be.

4. Alec Nove, The Soviet Economic System (London: George Allen and Unwin, 1977), p. 47.

5. Full and—they hope—efficient use of resources must be mandated by the planners since if they do not do it, no one else will. There is in the system no automatic mechanism for ensuring maxi-

mizing behavior in this sense, spontaneously on the part of economic
units. The planners' main way of going about this problem is to generate permanent resource tautness within the system.

6. Dimitri K. Simes, "The Soviet Parallel Market," in Economic
Aspects of Life in the USSR (Brussels: NATO Colloquium, May
1975), pp. 91–100; Gertrude E. Schroeder and Rush V. Greenslade,
"On the Measurement of the Second Economy in the USSR," ACES
Bulletin 21, no. 1 (Spring 1979): 3–19.

7. Joseph Watstein, "Soviet Economic Concessions: The
Agony and the Promise," ACES Bulletin 16, no. 1 (Spring 1974):
17–31.

8. "Most people devote their attention to the relationship of
the state and the provinces. I think that the essence lies in the relationship between the center (the state) and enterprises." Sun
Yehfang (rehabilitated Chinese economist), Interview with Yugoslav
News Agency Tanjug, Foreign Broadcast Information Service, August 28, 1978, pp. A26–A28.

9. Nove, op. cit., pp. 208–09. The optimum can be represented by several equilibrium points.

10. The centrally formulated managerial success indicators
in the Soviet Union in the mid- to late 1970s were roughly as shown
in the table below.

Generally Formulated Managerial Success Indicators

A. Physical

1. Output of the most important types of product
2. Share of top category in
   total output
3. Growth of labor productivity
4. Tasks for introduction and
   assimilation of new techniques
5. Tasks for reducing utilization norms of important
   inputs
6. Supply of key raw materials
   and equipment by superior
   agencies (material technical supply)

B. Financial

1. Sales volume of output
2. Profit
3. Profitability rates
   (rentabel'nost) computed as
   percentage of total capital,
   but also on occasion, of costs
4. Total wages fund
5. Prices of inputs and outputs.
   For collective farms, procurement prices for produce (quota
   and above quota)
6. Budgetary subsidies
7. Budgetary levies (turnover
   tax, capital charge, fixed
   rental payments, free re-
   mainder of profits)
8. Norms of payment into and out
   of enterprise stimulation
   funds

9. Investment from central funds
with specification of building
and installation
10. Completion of centralized
capital works
11. Norms of payment in respect
of capital assets and normed
working capital

11. Sun Yehfang, op. cit., "Correctly Applying the Law of
Value," Peking Review, No. 14 (April 6, 1979), pp. 14-16.
12. Campbell, op. cit., p. 39.
13. Average branch cost pricing means that some enterprises will be operating at a loss.
14. Soviet planners know the practical and theoretical usefulness of opportunity cost prices and they do occasionally try to construct such prices. See Campbell, op. cit., pp. 183-85.
15. Nove, op. cit., p. 178.
16. Jan Drewnowski, "The Economic Theory of Socialism:
A Suggestion for Reconsideration," Journal of Political Economy 69,
no. 4 (August 1961): 341-54.
17. Jan S. Prybyla, "Soviet Economic Reforms in Industry,"
Weltwirtschaftliches Archiv (Review of World Economics) 107, no. 2
(1971): 272-316; Joseph Berliner, The Innovation Decision in Soviet
Industry (Cambridge, Mass.: MIT Press, 1976), pp. 428-45; W. E.
Leeman, "Bonus Formulae and Soviet Managerial Performance,"
Southern Economic Journal, April 1972, pp. 434-45; M. L.
Weitzman, "The New Soviet Incentive Model," Bell Journal of Economics, Spring 1976, pp. 251-57.
18. William G. Rosenberg, "Observations on the Soviet Incentive System," ACES Bulletin 19, no. 3-4 (Fall-Winter 1977):
27-43.
19. Ibid., p. 35.
20. Robert W. Campbell, "Issues in Soviet R & D: The
Energy Case," in Soviet Economy in a New Perspective, Joint Economic Committee, Congress of the United States (Washington, D.C.:
U.S. Government Printing Office, 1976), pp. 97-112; Campbell,
The Soviet-Type Economies, op. cit., pp. 220-22.
21. Robert Wesson, "Why Soviet Economy Is Lagging,"
Business Week, February 26, 1979, p. 11.
22. Campbell, The Soviet-Type Economies, op. cit., pp.
221-22.
23. Gertrude E. Schroeder, "Soviet Economic Reform at an
Impasse," Problems of Communism, July-August 1971, pp. 36-46;
Gertrude E. Schroeder, "Soviet Economic Reforms: A Study in
Contradictions," Soviet Studies, July 1968, pp. 1-21.

24. Michael Ellman, <u>Soviet Planning Today: Proposals for an Optimally Functioning Economic System</u> (Cambridge: Cambridge University Press, 1971), p. 73, quoting Soviet economist A. N. Efimov: "Enormous practical difficulties are involved in going beyond first-order inputs for the determination of technical coefficients (production functions) even for key products." Nicholas Spulber, <u>The Soviet Economy: Structure, Principles, Problems</u>, rev. ed. (New York: W. W. Norton, 1969), pp. 22-23.

25. Campbell, <u>The Soviet-Type Economies</u>, op. cit., p. 189. Also pp. 186-89.

26. "It is utterly and totally impossible to collect information at the centre about micro-requirements and then convey the necessary orders to thousands of executant managers. No serious mathematical economist in the USSR pretends otherwise." Nove, op. cit., p. 53. ". . . in most instances <u>the centre does not know</u> just what it is that needs doing in disaggregated detail, while the management in its situation <u>cannot</u> know what it is that society needs unless the centre informs it." <u>Ibid.</u>, p. 86.

2
THE ECLIPSE OF MAOISM: CHANGES IN THE CHINESE ECONOMY AND THE QUEST FOR MODERNIZATION

REASONS FOR CHANGE

Since the purge of the Gang of Four in October 1976, but especially after the reinstatement of Deng Xiaoping, the Chinese press, radio, and television have carried fascinating accounts of what appear to be very important changes in the country's economy. The purpose of this chapter is to examine the meaning and significance of these changes, particularly as they affect the institutional structure of the economy.

There are two problems right at the start. First, it is not altogether clear what the economic record has been, for example, over the last dozen years or so. Those in power in Peking today paint a dismal picture of the economy between the beginning of Mao's Cultural Revolution in 1966 and the first quarter of 1977 when, according to all accounts, "initial great order" had been restored. Some of the troubles persisted as late as the last quarter of 1978. By contrast, many Western analyses of China's economy take a more positive view of the period, except for a bad year or two here and there (1968, 1974, and 1976, for example). Second, it is even less clear in which direction the economy is heading. Some reforms sound downright Stalinist (Stalin himself is cited now and then as a

─────────

This chapter was published earlier under the title "Changes in the Chinese Economy: An Interpretation," in Asian Survey 19, no. 5 (May 1979): 409-35. It is included here—with some minor additions and deletions—by permission of the editors of Asian Survey.

model of honesty and socialist probity); others look like watered-down versions of the sort of thing Liberman in Russia pushed in the early 1960s and that, with many an abortion, the Soviets are practicing today. Some observers say that they detect signs of a drift toward Yugoslav-type market socialism. What is clear is that big chunks of Maoist economic thought and practice are being torn from the structure of China's administrative command economy and that the demolition crews are in a big hurry. Why?

Because, it is alleged, the system that emerged from the Cultural Revolution (with its warmed-over institutional leftovers of the Great Leap) was not capable of modernizing China—at the very least, not fast enough.

There has been growth, of course, and there has been modernization both before and after the Cultural Revolution. If CIA estimates are to be believed, gross national product from 1952 through 1965 grew at an annual average rate of some 6 percent, the same yearly rate as from 1965 through 1976. Industrial output went up each year by between 9 and 10 percent, and agricultural production by 2 to 3 percent in both the periods 1952-1965 and 1965-1976. So obviously there was growth. There was also some modernization, quite a lot according to some.[1] In view of these changes, what's all the big fuss about? In this chapter I offer, for purposes of discussion, my interpretation of the meaning and significance of the changes being made in the structure of China's economy.

I think the growth that has occurred since the early 1960s has been extensive in the main, that is, brought about by the addition of, by and large, unimproved inputs of labor, capital, and land—especially labor.[2] The gauge of modernization was China's own recent past—more rarely, the contemporary condition of other developing countries. The time frame for reaching advanced world levels was generous; at least after the bitter lesson of the Great Leap had been absorbed. It would take China a hundred years, Mao wistfully predicted in 1962. The situation was particularly difficult in agriculture.[3]

Today the comparison with the most advanced countries is the spur to modernization (as it was at the beginning of the Great Leap). The time span has been shortened to the turn of the century; and the growth sought is intensive, that is, produced by increases in factor productivity. Such increases are to be brought about by technical-scientific improvement of the labor, capital, and land inputs—especially capital. The new venture may be aptly described as an intensive Great Leap Forward in contrast to its extensive predecessor of 1958-1959. Instead of applying huge amounts of raw muscle to the developmental problem, the new Leap's prescription is to hurl know-how and sophisticated capital equipment at the obstinate and elusive target.

The objectives of the modernization drive (the "new long march" as it is sometimes referred to in the official literature), together with target dates, are spelled out—albeit in very general terms—in the Outline Ten-Year Plan for the Development of the National Economy and its companion Outline Ten-Year Plan for the Development of Science and Technology. Both bear the imprint of Zhou Enlai and Deng Xiaoping. At this point all one need say is that the goals are very ambitious (some would say of epic proportions), capital- and skill-intensive, and tremendously costly. The cost and the sheer effort needed to raise skills and absorb the flood of intricate capital constitute what one might call the "objective" obstacles to the attainment of the goals. More disturbing are the persistent "subjective" difficulties in the way of target achievement: a widespread feeling that ranges from skepticism to outright hostility among some decision makers as well as a portion of the masses. Although again a hundred flowers have bloomed and contended, there is still, especially among middle and upper level cadres and the intellectuals, something approaching paranoia about a possible future settling of accounts and yet another round of persecutions. The voices from Peking are not unanimous, and the spiritual presence of the Gang has not yet been eliminated. The dangers of a backlash, especially in the event of the plan's failure, cannot be dismissed lightly.

It is said nowadays that before the Four were defrocked, the economy could not have reached the objectives set by the ten-year plans because it was shackled by several institutional so-called innovations engineered by the Gang—also, one may infer, by Mao himself, either intentionally or through neglect. There were, in other words, a number of built-in, systemic obstacles to intensive growth— Maoist additions to the original Soviet-like structure of China's administrative command economy. It is fair to point out that while Chairman Mao was alive and in fair functioning condition, these very parts of the economic edifice were described as creative additions to the organizational principles and grand design of Marxism-Leninism.

The systemic obstacles to modernization stemming from Mao's perspective on events and his idiosyncratic approach to the resolution of practical problems may be identified as being five in number. I shall label them priorities, self-reliance, motivation, innovation, and planning.

Priorities

By "priorities" I mean the ranking of societal objectives and economic sectors on the planners' scale of preferences. An important characteristic of Maoism is its preoccupation with the objective of equity and its placing of equity above growth on the scale of social priorities. Equity is taken to mean "justice" in the distribution of goods and services (money and in-kind income flows and stocks); power (the capacity to influence the behavior of others or the negative capacity to prevent others from influencing one's behavior); and opportunity at the start. Justice, in this context, means less inequality. I think there is a strong egalitarian streak to the Maoist creed, always restrained by an inherited Leninist organizational elitism. This egalitarian compulsion manifested itself repeatedly during Mao's lifetime in three policy areas: wages, cadre privileges, and education. The first and last will be discussed at greater length later. Here we note only that a key purpose of the Cultural Revolution was to shake up the privileged bureaucratic stratum, make the power-holders lose face, "drag" them down to the level of the masses, and compel them to share their power in various three-in-one committees and other participatory formations. It is important not to exaggerate the distance traveled on the egalitarian road under Mao's helmsmanship because Marxist-Leninist societies are inherently inegalitarian when it comes to the distribution of power. However, it was quite a stretch; much longer than the distance traveled by the Soviets at roughly an equivalent stage in their economic development.

Now it can be argued (and will be so argued under the headings Motivation and Innovation below) that the process of modernization calls for far-reaching violations of equity. Someone has to be in charge, responsibility must be personalized, too much leveling—especially leveling down—saps the "production enthusiasm" of the more skilled workers, and so on. In short, growth (creation of wealth) and equity (redistribution of wealth) do on occasion collide.

Maoist preoccupation with income redistribution is matched by Maoism's preference for asceticism. Asceticism, at least the sackcloth side of it, is brought about by a low wages policy. It is true that low wages ("low" compared with the prices of everything except physically rationed rockbottom necessities) may be seen as an objective necessity at the present stage of China's development, a means of curbing consumption and assuring the economy's ability to form capital at the desired rates. However, Maoism seems to regard asceticism and its parent low wages policy subjectively, as praiseworthy per se. This is not, I think, just making virtue of necessity. Attachment to the Spartan ideal is second nature to Maoism. It exists independently of any objective resource constraint. This attitude, too, constitutes a possible hindrance to growth, especially "modern" intensive growth that multiplies output per man-hour, improves the capital/output ratio, and raises not only yields per hectare but the consumers' horizon of expectations.

Agriculture in the new China has never been exploited like Soviet agriculture had been under Stalin, but until 1958 it played second fiddle to industry, especially heavy industry. After the Great Leap agriculture was raised to the number one spot on the planners' preference scale, light industry came second, and heavy industry (with the possible exception of agricultural support industries) was third. In the setting of a largely self-reliant economy, this sectoral ranking meant that the rate of the economy's growth was determined in large part by the growth of agricultural production.

Self-Reliance

The Maoist doctrine of self-reliance has at least four origins: a fairly natural propensity of large continental powers to rely primarily on their own resources; China's unfortunate experience with foreign economic relations in the nineteenth and early twentieth centuries, and later with the Soviets; habits acquired during communism's guerrilla days; and China's millenial self-centeredness and instinctive suspicion of and disdain for things foreign.

The relevance of self-reliance to modernization, as modernization is understood now, is both external and domestic. Externally, it is said, self-reliance as preached by the Gang hindered the inflow from abroad of advanced technology both in the form of know-how and fixed assets. To catch up with the most advanced countries in a brief span of time, China must import large quantities of scientific and technical information and some very sophisticated and costly equipment. Adherence to the doctrine of self-reliance has meant four things in practice:

Foreign trade was regarded as a residual activity to be resorted to only when absolutely necessary.

Foreign trade turnover was depressed below its potential by the conservative policy of having overall imports and exports balance preferably each year, but if that proved impractical, within 2 or 3 years at the outside.

There was active avoidance of long-term indebtedness toward foreigners (banks and governments); this meant that longer-term developmental credits were not sought and joint ventures were taboo.

The number and scope of scientific and technical personnel exchanges between China and other countries was small. In fact, China gave more technical advice to developing countries than it received from the developed ones.

Internally, self-reliance has meant the sacrifice of benefits flowing from regional comparative advantage and the division of labor. It has encouraged the formation of "all-embracing organizations [both] big and small, [which] are a backward form of organization," and pushed the economy in a cellular direction.

Motivation

The work force has to be set in motion, efficiently if possible. Modern scientific and technical knowledge will be wasted if managers and workers are not properly motivated or are motivated in perverse ways. The problem is twofold: incentives to management and incentives to labor (workers, peasants, employees). It is claimed that during the Gang's rule the managerial function was seriously undermined:

In the name of democratization the (Leninist-Stalinist) directorial principle, which stresses hierarchies within the firm and one-man responsibility, was abolished and replaced by three-way Revolutionary Committees composed of rehabilitated cadres, technicians, and representatives of the masses. These committees (one of the "newborn socialist things" issuing from the Cultural Revolution) were prone to factionalism, worked at cross purposes with party committees, and quickly turned into political battlegrounds. As a result of the quality of management suffered, production stagnated, and productivity declined in many industrial plants and farms.

Managers were reluctant to practice economic accounting for fear of being accused of putting material production forces before correct politics, or of trying to befuddle the masses with figures.[4] Profit, especially, became a dirty word. It could be argued that the damage done to the economy through sloppy cost accounting was not great because the Chinese price and cost structure does not even remotely reflect relative scarcities (the wage structure, for example, has not changed in over 20 years). Not everyone agrees with this assessment, yet it seems, to me at least, highly plausible.

Many rules and regulations essential to the orderly conduct of business affairs were thrown out on the contention that they were elitist. As a result labor discipline became unglued: absenteeism was reportedly rampant, on-the-job performance became something less than exemplary, attention to the quantity and quality of output was minimal, industrial safety was neglected, and so forth. Thomas Robinson, who visited one particular factory before the Gang's fall, was told proudly that "in the old [Liuist] days we the workers had to punch in and punch out. All that is now done away with."[5] The punch clock, it is now said, was apparently replaced by a visitor's book.

Managers and key technical personnel were being reeducated in May 7th schools and through manual labor. Whatever the class benefits of this moving around, it, too, can be pushed to the point where managerial professionalism falls victim to the trade school mentality.

The spread between managerial salaries and the upper grades of production workers' wages was relatively narrow with, no doubt, disincentive effects on managerial effort; managerial bonuses were suppressed, and the top salaries were either trimmed or phased out upon retirement of the office holders.

Enterprise choice-making latitude was severely restricted by the enterprise's obligation to surrender all profits to the state treasury. Even as late as April 1978, giving all profits to the state was described as the "glorious duty of a socialist enterprise."

The following measures may be seen as having had disincentive effects on industrial and, more generally, nonagricultural workers and employees:

The general level of wages had remained unchanged for over 20 years, while increases in industrial labor productivity are thought to have been 1-1.5 percent a year during that period.[6] The average annual rate of increase in the urban retail price index from 1952 through 1971 is believed to have been under 1 percent.[7] So, overt inflation was not a problem. However, after 20 years the workers were ready for some marginal improvement in consumption and were not as enthusiastic about the "moral" (that is, low-wage) economy as some Western visitors to China.

Under the impact of radical left philosophy, wage differentials were compressed to the point where the more skilled workers in the upper range of the eight-grade industrial wage scale became restive. There was also (and still is) a significant overlap between the wages of the higher paid production workers and the lower ranges of the technicians' salary scale. This, too, tends to have disincentive effects on people with specialized technical training. At present, postliberation college graduates who have worked the longest receive, on the average, a monthly wage of not more than 100 yuan, which is about the same as the average wage of upper-grade production workers. Recent college graduates get up to 40 yuan a month on the average—which is just about what the lower-paid production workers earn. That is also probably what these graduates are worth.

The climate of official opinion was against seniority in the work place and in favor of the raw young recruit politically tempered by the Cultural Revolution but who had little going for him in the way of skill or even half-decent education. Such a working environment had, no doubt, adverse repercussions on both the senior worker's performance and discipline among the lower ranks.

The morale of senior and, more generally, regular industrial workers was eroded by the presence in factories of temporary workers. The latter were not covered by social security, worked at low pay to keep their factory jobs, and generally acted as the socialist equivalent of Marx's "reserve army of the unemployed." The pre-Cultural Revolution labor unions—the membership of which was made up of regular workers—were apparently unhappy about the arrangement. The unions were put on the back burner during the Cultural Revolution and began to stir again only around 1973. [8]

Bonuses, overtime pay, and piecework were abolished. Extra work was expected as a matter of correct proletarian consciousness. The emphasis shifted to collective moral incentives: little red flags and stars for workshops and teams stuck on the factory wall. In a book (Socialist Political Economy) published in Shanghai under the Gang's auspices, piecework pay and bonuses were described as "insults to the working class" and "counterrevolutionary acts."

There was a distinct absence of "socialist legality." Under the ancien regime, it is now argued, there was widespread capriciousness in the treatment of enterprises by higher echelons of the state bureaucracy. As Hu Chiao-mu describes it, plan indicators were changed at will, "certain leading bodies according to their whim [ordered] peasants to uproot crops they had planted and grow other crops instead, without being responsible both legally and economically for the ensuing losses," many production teams' accounting and income distribution functions were arbitrarily transferred to the brigades, team labor was conscripted for brigade or commune work without regard to the teams' farming needs and often without proper compensation, contracts remained unfulfilled and unenforced, and so on. In brief, where the interests of the state and the enterprise failed to coincide, the interest of the enterprise was almost invariably sacrificed. This had negative effects on enterprise efficiency. There was also endemic violation of "socialist legality" with regard to the individual worker's and peasant's right of person. The peasants' household plots and their personal rights (for example, the right to sell surplus produce from the plots on the free market) were "placed at the free disposal of higher-up levels, of certain leader or leaders, including the individual cadres of a commune, production brigade or production team," and the legitimate organs of authority (for example, meetings of commune members' delegates at all levels) were "ignored altogether." Subsumed in all this rampant illegality was the oppression in the villages of people belonging to the "incorrect categories." In short, where the interests of the enterprise and the individual member of the enterprise failed to coincide, the individual interest, it is said, was invariably jettisoned.

The general level of in-kind and money income from collective work is now said to have remained unchanged for 20 years. "With the exception of the better areas, the income of the peasants, after a year's work, shows little or no increase at all in many places, although production has gone up; in a few places incomes have actually decreased with the increase in production. The reasons for this are manifold. . . ." One reason frequently cited these days was agriculture's adverse terms of trade with industry, that is, farm incomes were depressed by a combination of low prices paid by the state for agricultural produce and high prices paid by farms for industrial goods. Over the years price parities have shifted somewhat in favor of agriculture: state procurement prices (prices paid by the state for compulsory and above-quota deliveries of farm produce) doubled "in the last 20 years and more since the founding of the People's Republic," while retail prices of industrial goods rose by only 28 percent. However, the disparity between the two "is still fairly large at present."[9] Other reasons probably included high compulsory delivery quotas at the state fixed prices, excessive deductions for the capital fund, and perhaps an agricultural tax more burdensome that was commonly admitted, partly because—despite assurances to the contrary—the rate of the tax was apparently not fixed for long periods but was subject to often capricious changes at short notice.[10]

Peasant workpoint incentive systems were also weakened by the introduction of increasingly egalitarian methods of income distribution. (How widespread the practice was it is difficult to say.) Apparently the effect was most strongly felt by the better farms and the comparatively well-off peasants in suburban communes.

Innovation

The reverse side of self-reliance is the capacity of the self-reliant society to come up with advanced scientific and technical innovations. It could be argued that the Gang of Four (Five, if Mao is included) erected three obstacles in the path of the needed domestic innovation. These may be listed as the "red versus expert" dilemma, educational reform, and the choice of technologies.

The red versus expert dialectic as interpreted by the Gang meant persecution of intellectuals—branded "white" by definition. Indeed, a virulent antiintellectualism is one of Maoism's less engaging characteristics. From another perspective, red versus expert meant the elevation of "politics"—Mao lore—to commander of all work, brain work included. The intellectuals were dumped into the "stinking ninth" category.

The Cultural Revolution's educational reform downgraded "book learning" and pure research compared with learning by doing; wiped out graduate study; opened the universities to the class-correct but often intellectually dull offspring of the red classes; drastically simplified curricula; and shortened periods of study. Militant worker and peasant supervisory teams were permanently stationed in the schools to keep an eye on things and stamp out the slightest deviation from the line. The reform reduced China's educational system to a shambles.

Maoism's technological preference was for "walking on two legs," that is, to use simultaneously advanced capital- and skill-intensive and semitraditional, labor-intensive technology. Actually, semitraditional ("intermediate") technology was the favorite, much of it the product of mass peasant and worker inventiveness. It was a matter of emphasis rather than of mutually exclusive alternatives. Capital-intensive large-scale industrialization was not neglected, but for a variety of reasons local, small- and medium-scale, labor-intensive industrialization was preferred.

Planning

During the reign of the Gang of Four both the practice and theory of macro planning were neglected. The periods of supremacy of Maoist thought in the realm of practice—the Great Leap Forward and the Cultural Revolution—were periods of planlessness. The essence of a Soviet-type administrative command economy, of which China is an example, is that it lacks an automatic information-gathering, processing, and conveying mechanism. Goal formulation and resource allocation are deliberate, conscious processes. If the planners don't do it, it doesn't get done. The whole tenor of Maoist teaching, with its emphasis on the importance of the political will and its obsession with constant movement, confrontation, and upheaval, is inimical to the planning process, which calls for orderly process, routine, and a measure of stability.

Maoism—it is alleged—neglected the theory of central planning. This theory has two main components: study of physical planning (physical indicators and technical coefficients, input-output tables, material balances, coefficients of investment effectiveness, and so on), and study of pricing in the conditions of socialism. These two components are sometimes referred to in communist terminology as, respectively, the "law of planned, proportional development of the national economy," and the "law of value." "Planning comes first, and prices second. This calls for first drawing up plans in accordance with social needs; the next thing is to set rational prices for various products, and to see that these prices serve our plans, rather than separating the two."[11] In the intellectual atmosphere created by the Cultural Revolution it was imprudent, to say the least, to advocate learning about socialist economic laws, especially the law of value.

THE TEN-YEAR MODERNIZATION PLAN

Individually and collectively, it is now argued, these five systemic obstacles made it very unlikely that the objectives set in the ten-year plans could have been reached in the time span reserved for them. In fact, had these five evils been allowed to grow, there would have been no ten-year plans and no modernization of the type and scope now envisioned.

To grasp what is envisioned, let us take a quick glance at the major targets of the ten-year plans. For the sake of brevity we shall limit ourselves to the targets set for agriculture and industry.

Agriculture

The major quantifiable agricultural goals can be listed under two headings: production and inputs. Production of grain is to reach 400 million metric tons in 1985, 43 percent above the estimated 280 million tons of 1977. From 1978 through 1985 the value of agricultural output is to rise by 4-5 percent per year (compared with 2.8 percent per year over 1949-1976, and 2.4 percent over 1970-1976). By 1985 there is to be 1 mou (one-fifteenth of a hectare) of farmland with guaranteed stable high yields per member of the rural population. By the year 2000 output per hectare of the major farm products is to reach or surpass advanced world levels. In 1977 the grain yield per hectare was about 2,000 kilograms. It is hoped that by 1985, one-third of China's farmland will have grain yields of 15,000 kilograms per hectare.

From 1978 through 1985 state investment in farm capital construction (leveling, terracing, drainage, irrigation) will be equivalent to the total state investment from 1949 through 1977. If Soochow

Prefecture, Jiangsu, is any guide, the cost of the operation is likely to be about $1,000 a hectare—altogether about $35 billion.[12] The state will take charge of large-scale water conservancy projects, including the harnessing of the Yellow, Yangtze, Huai, Haiho, Liaoho, and Pearl rivers and the diversion of 30 billion cubic meters of water a year from the Yangtze River to areas both south and north of the Yellow River. By 1985 a total of 13 million hectares of wasteland will be reclaimed. From 1949 through 1977 China reclaimed 17 million hectares of land, or roughly 0.6 million hectares a year. To reach the 1985 target, the annual addition from 1978 through 1985 will have to be nearly three times that.[13] Annual chemical fertilizer output in 1979 was double the 1977 figure, while the plan foresaw only a 58 percent increase. By 1980 tractors are to number an estimated 2 million compared with 1.2 million in 1976, and the proportion of large and medium-sized tractors in the total is to rise. According to my calculations all this will mean that by 1980, if all goes well, there will be roughly one tractor (in 15-horsepower units) for every 100 hectares of arable land. By 1980 machine-drawn farm implements are to increase by 110 percent over 1977, hand-guided tractors by 36 percent. Supplies of steel from the state for production and repair of farm machinery in 1978-1980 are to increase by 60 percent over 1975-1977, while the proportion of steel supplied by local authorities for the same purpose is scheduled to rise to 40 percent of total supplies from the current 30 percent. Between 1978 and 1980 the state was to increase deliveries of gasoline and lubricants to agriculture 1.2 times. In 1980 the number of personnel capable of operating, maintaining, repairing, and managing farm machines should be double that of 1977. By 1980 over 90 percent of farm machines are to be in good working condition and the rate of utilization of farm machines is to exceed 80 percent. Quality problems connected with the construction, use, and upkeep of farm machines have apparently been serious in the past. These included too little standardization and serialization (my observation was that many tractors were custom made), shortages of spare parts—a perennial socialist problem—and poor maintenance of machines on the farms (shortage of qualified mechanics and repair facilities). Many machines delivered to the farms were lemons. "The peasants complained: 'We sold our live oxen to buy iron oxen [tractors], but what we got were dead oxen.'"[14] By 1980 the cost to the farms of farm machinery will be lowered by one-fifth from the 1977 cost. By 1985 compulsory eight-year education is to be generalized in the countryside and a system of agrotechnical stations is to be set up and expanded.

Parallel to the agricultural plan is the objective of reducing the natural rate of population growth to less than 1 percent by 1980.

Industry

Here, too, the convenient expositional breakdown is between production and inputs. Between 1976 and 1985 the average annual growth rate of industrial output is to be 10 percent, which is the same as the estimated realized average annual growth rate over the period 1965-1975. Ignoring the early recovery years (1949-1952) when production rose quickly from very low levels, the fastest average annual growth rate of industrial output was registered between 1953 and 1957 (First Five-Year Plan) when it was 16 percent. The projected rate is achievable and likely to be exceeded by a substantial margin. That figure is likely to be raised in view of the sharp increase in industrial production in 1978. In 1979 industrial output increased by 6.4 percent over the preceding year. By 1985 coal production is to be twice what it had been in 1977, that is, it is to reach 1 billion metric tons. The 1985 output is to come increasingly from large mechanized mines, whereas in 1977 roughly one-third of production originated in small, labor-intensive mines. In 1985 steel production was projected to reach 60 million metric tons (34.5 million in 1979). By that date ten new Daqing-like oilfields were to be discovered, implying the location of onshore oil reserves of at least 4-5 billion tons, equivalent to the estimated present onshore reserves. Offshore exploration is to be vigorously pursued. It is counted on not only to provide large additional reserves (estimated at 10-20 billion tons), but to ease onshore bottlenecks caused by insufficiency of pipelines, overloading of railroads, and overcrowded storage and port facilities. These can be eased by using the single-point buoy mooring system of loading crude oil directly into tankers at the offshore field. In the development of electric power, hydroelectricity is to play the leading role. From 1978 to 1985 the total amount of major products produced by the machine-building industry is to exceed the total for 1949-1977. Sixty complete sets of large equipment are to be built by 1985. Consumer goods production is to be expanded and the quality of the goods is to improve.[15] There is something for everyone in the package.*

The original plan envisaged the construction of 120 large industrial complexes. Included were 10 iron and steel combines, 9 nonferrous metals complexes, 8 coal mines, 10 oil and gas fields, 30 large electric power stations, 6 new trunk railroads (presumably including three high speed corridors totaling 2,300 miles), and 5 key

*The plan was considerably trimmed in the winter of 1978. (See Prybyla, "China in the 1980s," Challenge, May-June 1980, pp. 4-20.)

harbors. Industries new or comparatively new to China are to be established with foreign assistance. Included are polymer synthesis, nuclear power, electronic computers, lasers, semiconductors, and astronautics.

The price tags on these projects keep coming in and rising. The total cost of importing foreign technology (know-how and plant equipment) from 1976 through 1985 is tentatively put at $40-50 billion, and the guess is probably on the low side.

In late 1978 it became increasingly clear that the Chinese government was pulling in the reins and scaling down its ambitions. Japanese firms received notices from Peking informing them that an agreement on Japan's cooperation in the construction of an integrated steel mill at Baoshan had not yet taken effect. The reason given was that no agreement had so far been reached on loans to help finance the project. China has insisted that credit arrangements, including the financing of bilateral trade, be made in U.S. dollars rather than Japanese yen, the Chinese being concerned about the appreciation of the yen against the dollar. Similar notices were received by other Japanese companies doing business with China, while several ongoing negotiations (for example, about joint development of oil deposits in the Gulf of Bohai) ground to a halt. In all, China concluded in 1978 some 49 plant purchase contracts with Japan. The deals that the Chinese subsequently declared to be noneffectual came to 420 billion yen, with the Baoshan contract representing more than half that amount. The ten-year plan was much trimmed by the Third Plenary Session of the party's Eleventh Central Committee, held in December 1978. Although not abandoned, the plan was "readjusted" to make it more attractive and internally consistent. A Three-Year Plan (1978-1980) of "Readjustment, Transformation, Consolidation, and Improvement" was announced.

SOLUTIONS FOR OBSTACLES
TO MODERNIZATION

Our interest here is not so much with whether China can make it financially, but with whether the institutions of the Chinese economy, as they emerge from the prolonged two-line struggle, are strong and flexible enough to carry the burden implied in the accounting and physics of the plan. Specifically, we want to take another look at the alleged five systemic obstacles to modernization and see what is being done about them.

Priorities

What has happened to the planners' ranking of objectives and sectors since the demise of the Four? There has been a sharp shift in the ranking of objectives. The possibility of a conflict between growth and equity is openly recognized and growth comes out the winner. Growth at rapid rates is now the number one societal objective to which all must give way. Equity in the distribution of goods and services, power, and opportunity at the start has been demoted. While the policy of low wages is to continue, it is to be mitigated and eventually got rid of. Mitigation assumes four forms: there will be occasional, rather modest, general wage increases; the opprobrium attached by the radicals to the consumption of "trivia" (for example, clothes of any color other than basic blue or green) has been removed; residential housing is to be improved; and a greater volume of foreign goods has been made available in the shops, at least in the larger cities. In short, asceticism is no longer regarded as a revolutionary virtue; it is now called by its old name, "poverty." Low consumption is diagnosed as an unpleasantness necessitated by the process of capital accumulation. The dragging down of power holders and intellectuals for the sheer fun of it—a favorite indoor and outdoor sport of the radicals—has been replaced (again) by the tactics of the united front and the careful building up of the authority of middle and upper echelon bureaucrats, scientists, and academics. Overseas Chinese dependents are again in good graces. All this change runs counter to the objective of narrowing down power and income differentials. We shall see later that a similar elitist trend exists in the once more reformed educational system.

In a strictly formal sense there has been no change in the planners' sectoral priorities. Agriculture remains the "foundation" of the national economy, and industry the "leading factor." Within industry, the ranking remains as it was: light followed by heavy industry. However, a discreet shift has taken place in favor of industry in general and heavy industry in particular. The stress on modern industrial capital and massive scale of operations and the staggering sums involved in the expansion and modernization of basic industrial branches (coal, oil, electricity, iron and steel, machine building) overshadow even the most grandiose capital construction projects in agriculture. The new temper is urban as contrasted with the Maoist fascination with rural areas. There is, however, no indication so far of a Stalinist drift. Agriculture is not to be exploited for the sake of industry, but it has to shape up. In sum, the post-Gang sectoral priorities are more "orthodox" in the sense of current Soviet-type orthodoxy.

Self-Reliance

The Gang, it is now said, distorted the meaning of self-reliance. Economically they confused self-reliance with autarky, and politically with xenophobis, which could only result in China's eventual international isolation. Externally, it is now argued, China must rely on the industrially advanced countries for the supply of up-to-date scientific, technical, and managerial know-how and capital equipment. Without too much fear the new China might also, it is suggested, learn something from foreigners' consumption habits. Domestically, there is need to deemphasize "integrated, self-contained" regions, branches, and enterprises and stress greater geographical and functional interdependence.

The major changes in the external application of the self-reliance doctrine have been the following:

Foreign trade has become the key link in the chain of modernization. Even when the Gang was around (1965-1976), foreign trade grew at an average annual rate of 12 percent (18 percent from 1970 through 1976). This rate is to be accelerated. To facilitate the expansion of foreign commerce new foreign trade companies are being established; their function is to coordinate the work of the existing state trading corporations with the needs of production units involved in the export-import business. Some discretion to deal with foreign businesses has been delegated by the center to provincial and lower authorities. This has been accompanied by a doubling of foreign exchange allocations to local production units for the purchase of foreign equipment.

The conservative policy that sought to balance exports and imports or produce a surplus of exports over imports on the trade account over fairly short spans of time is being cautiously liberalized. The magnitude of the planned imports makes it practically certain that the import bill cannot be met from current commodity exports only—at least not by 1985. To ease pressures on commodity exports, China has taken steps to increase service exports, particularly tourism. Chinese investments in lucrative Hong Kong projects (including hotels and real estate) have risen sharply in 1978.

There are no longer serious inhibitions about accepting long-term loans from foreign banks and loans or loan guarantees from foreign government-related agencies such as Export-Import Banks (Japan, United States) and the British Export Credit Guarantee Department. The progression has been in six steps: acceptance of seller-arranged deferred payments; of foreign bank deposits in branches of the Bank of China; of project-related foreign bank loans; of syndicated international credits; of bank loans unrelated to specific projects (purely financial borrowing); and of government-to-government loans. In another break with the past, China has approached a number of United Nations agencies (for example, the UN Development Program, the World Health Organization, UNESCO) regarding the possibility of loans to help finance, among other objectives, foreign language training in China. The old taboos that surrounded joint ventures are crumbling fast. Joint ventures are of two kinds: coproduction arrangements involving either payment of specified portion of the product to the foreign partner or a profit sharing agreement (the profit being shared in kind or cash or both); and equity participation arrangements. Both kinds of joint ventures are now legitimized by China. According to Vice Premier Li Xiannian (July 7, 1979), China will not confine herself to limiting the foreign share to 49 percent of total joint venture capital. The proportion of investment by foreign companies can be higher than 50 percent, and the duration may be ten years, 20 years, or even longer. A law on joint ventures was adopted by the Second Session of the Fifth National People's Congress on July 1, 1979.[16]

The number and scope of scientific and technical personnel exchanges between China and other countries is to rise dramatically in the next few years. While reciprocity is bruited about, the prospect is for perhaps ten times as many Chinese coming to study in the West as Westerners going to study in China.

Internally, the tendency to create all-embracing, self-contained economic regions and units (ministerial branches, individual enterprises, communes, or brigades) is now decried as wasteful duplication. Perhaps the decision announced by Hua to recreate the six regional economic authorities that cut across provincial administrative boundaries may be seen as an attempt to dilute local geopolitical autarkies. Although Dazhai and Daqing—both models of all-round self-reliance—have been in the news a lot since the fall of the Gang, the "all-roundedness" (self-sufficiency) component of their experience has been deemphasized of late in line with the new stress on specialization and interdependence. By mid-1979 Dazhai was hardly mentioned any more.

Motivation

The incentive problem, it will be recalled, is twofold: incentives to management and incentives to labor (workers, peasants, employees). Let us see what changes have been made in the motivational system under both subheadings. As regards incentives to management:

The directorial principle, with its emphasis on hierarchies within the firm and one-man responsibility under party committee supervision, has been restored and revolutionary committees have been abolished. The current system (still in the making) consists of an enterprise party committee elected every two years by party members within the enterprise and headed by a party secretary assisted by deputy secretaries and several members; a working committee (managerial board) headed by the enterprise director assisted by deputy directors and responsible technical-administrative cadres; and—in some places—a "workers' (or people's) supervision group" under the leadership of the party committee, representing workers and staff members. This group (which in the case of retail stores may include representatives of the public and of suppliers) holds regular meetings (every 2 or 3 months) and acts as a structured organ for checking up at the grassroots of the enterprise. The basic policy decisions are made by the party committee; day-to-day managerial and technical matters are handled by the director and his working committee; and, to lend the system a vaguely participatory appeal, the workers' supervision group under the party's supervision makes sure that the state's plan is properly carried out. It is argued that the present system differs from the "Soviet" one practiced during the 1950s in that the powers of the enterprise director are more restricted, and the powers of the party committee are by comparison wider. On the other hand, compared with the managerial arrangements issuing from the Cultural Revolution, the present system gives more power to the enterprise director and his staff than was ever wielded by the chairman of the revolutionary committee, and—through the tight structuring of worker involvement under close party supervision—it takes some power away from the rank-and-file workers and employees. In short, the current system is not too different from the one that operated under Liu Shaoqi from the early 1960s until the outbreak of the Cultural Revolution.

Enterprise economic accounting has been rehabilitated. Profit, profitability, cost accounting, and enterprise accountability (what the Soviets call khozraschet) are insisted on, with all sorts of administrative, financial, and criminal punishments reserved for noncompliance. There is talk of letting enterprises retain a portion of their profits (an innovation) and setting up enterprise funds out of these retained profits.[17] The idea is to have three such funds: one for material incentives (bonuses) to "advanced workers" including managerial staffs, one for social-cultural purposes, and one for enterprise investments ("production development") outside the state plan. The proposal is reminiscent of what had been introduced in the Soviet Union by the industrial reforms of the late 1960s. Disbursement out of the funds would be made by the director, presumably with the approval of the party committee and in consonance with ministerial or other higher-echelon regulations.

As part of general formalization of procedures (insistence on clearly articulated and enforced "socialist legality"), enterprise discipline has been tightened up. Enforcement of labor discipline is apparently one of the functions of the newly revitalized trade unions.

Although cadre participation in manual labor continues to be talked about as "one of the basic principles laid down by Chairman Mao for running socialist enterprises," the talk does not ring true. It may be presumed that under the new dispensation, May 7th school-type interruptions of managerial routine will become much less frequent than in former years. One of the problems plaguing China's industry, one moreover to which the Cultural Revolution has significantly contributed, is the comparatively low quality of managerial and technical personnel, two-thirds of whom joined the factories since 1968, and most of whom have had little professional training. Reinstatement of engineers and managers who in past years had been sent down to the factory floor is being carried out in the face of opposition from former Cultural Revolutionaries who fear that once reinstated these people will take revenge, and also because there is a widespread feeling that if these men are taken away from the production line, the workshops will not function properly.

Managerial bonuses are to be reestablished. Recent wage and salary increases do not appear to have widened the fairly narrow gap between managerial salaries and the upper grades of production workers' wages. However, managerial power incomes have certainly improved since the fall of the Gang.

It is not clear yet how far, if at all, the decision-making powers of enterprises will be enlarged. The present discussion seems to revolve around two issues: whether enterprises should be permitted to retain a portion of the profits they make and use these monies for certain specified purposes (including off-plan investments); and to what extent enterprises should be permitted to enter directly into contracts with one another. In the meantime under the "30-Point Decision on Industry" issued by the Central Committee of the Communist Party of China in 1978 the number of centrally fixed enterprise norms ("success indicators") has been raised from five to eight, with the possibility of a ninth (amount of fixed assets to be used by an enterprise) being added in the future. (The nine centrally determined indicators are not very different from those fixed by Soviet planners for their enterprises.) While there are certainly crosscurrents in the debate about the degree of enterprise autonomy, there seems to be a fair measure of agreement that in agriculture, at least, the basic producing and accounting unit—the production team—should be granted greater latitude to manage its own affairs.

A number of steps have been taken to improve incentives to workers, peasants, and employees:

A general increase in wages was decreed effective October 1, 1977. The increase applied to 60 percent of industrial workers, workers and staff in the commercial and service trades, teachers, scientific, technical, medical, literary, and art workers, and government functionaries. About 46 percent of the workers and employees received increases in the wage rates applicable to their particular job grade. Another 18 percent were moved up the job grade ladder because "they had been classified too low for their jobs." "Generally" the wage increase was of the order of 10 percent. While the raises were said to have benefited primarily those earning less than 90 yuan a month, workers with many years of experience (that is, with seniority and presumably better pay) were also included. Views of coworkers were apparently sought in deciding whose wages should be raised, but the final determination was made by party committees. It was revealed that state expenditures on labor insurance and other social benefits came to 10 percent of the total wages bill. The incentive effect of money wage increases will, of course, depend on the willingness and ability of the planners to channel resources into light industry so as to increase the volume and enlarge the assortment of consumer goods. Such a commitment has been made, but it may be difficult to implement in view of the competing claims of other sectors and industries, particularly the defense industry. However, some mileage may be got out of removing the hostility toward consumption that was part of the Gang's ethic, at least on the rhetorical plane. Many goods and services can be made available without much shifting of resources simply by lifting the ban on their use and display. Already the variety of cultural fare has been improved by the inexpensive expedient of letting different art forms compete for the public's attention and allowing books authored by others than Mao to be sold in the stores.

Wage differentials are likely to become wider if only because of the new stress on seniority and professionalism, and the restoration of bonuses, which have a way of accruing mostly to higher-grade workers. "The wage spread," says Renmin Ribao (May 5, 1978), "may be readjusted rationally." Exceptionally talented people will be promoted rapidly and need not necessarily climb the wage ladder rung by rung. There is the possibility that, given the enormous investments in urban-based plant and equipment (which presumably will result in significant gains in labor productivity), the urban-rural income gap, wide though it is, will become even greater. This gap may pose rural-urban migration problems, especially in the event the rustication movement is discontinued and there is retreat from the hitherto practiced administrative allocation of labor.

The climate of official opinion has shifted in favor of experienced, skilled, senior workers. The offspring of the Cultural Revolution are now depicted, if not in so many words, as intellectually crippled and emotionally unstable. The problem is delicate and potentially explosive. The modernizers cannot afford to alienate millions of young people who had been educationally disadvantaged by the Cultural Revolution and embittered by subsequent events. To brush them aside would aggravate China's already formidable generation-gap problem and invite trouble in the future. The unruly and cynical products of the Cultural Revolution have to be associated in the task of modernization and given a sense of participation and personal worth. Failure to do this would build up a disgruntled constituency responsive to the lures of the opposition to the current line.

The problem of temporary workers antedates the Cultural Revolution. Not much is known about the dimensions and details of the problem except that it is persistent and causes friction within factories. It is not clear whether anything is being done about it. One would presume that the unions—now revived again—which have never been happy with the situation, will try to intervene in some way.

Bonuses, overtime pay, various allowances (for example, for haircuts, commuting, extra nutrition when working under comparatively difficult conditions), overtime pay, and piecework have been restored. The general characteristics of the system are as follows. First, as compared with the "Liuist" period (1961-1965) the system is said to be less complex and the bonuses more modest (Western observers consider them too low to have any significant incentive impact). Second, compared with the "Liuist" period, differentiated bonuses are not paid directly to individuals, but to the enterprise's workshops and work teams. They are awarded for the fulfillment of norms set by the state plan, for example, the norms for volume of output, consumption of raw and semifinished materials, quality, and so on. These awards are made monthly by the enterprise. Every workshop then holds an "appraisal session" (attended by the party branch secretary and his deputy, the workshop director and his deputy, the workshop statistician, and team leaders) at which workers in each team are reviewed. Every member of a team that

has fulfilled its state norms and been awarded a bonus will receive
an equal bonus provided he has fulfilled his norm for, say, atten-
dance. While before the Cultural Revolution, one is told, the Kailan
coal mines had as many as 70 different kinds of bonus and the sums
involved were so large that some workers' bonuses added up to
more than those workers' basic wage, it is probable that the present
system—still at a trial stage—sins on the side of simplicity, egali-
tarianism, and insufficient amounts. "There are several workers
who think that the method of giving awards to the collective should
be improved, because giving an equal bonus for every team does not
fully accord with the principle 'to each according to his work.'"
Third, bonuses to production workers and cadres at or below the
workshop level are counted as part of the cost of production, in the
same way as in the Soviet Union. They represent roughly 10 percent of the wages bill. Fourth, while time-work rates of pay are
most common, piecework has been reintroduced in certain branches,
for example, in the loading and unloading of ships. "In the present
circumstances when wages are low, payment by piece serves as a
premium and a socialist incentive that has no negligible function in
improving the life of the masses."[18]

Two trends are detectable as regards the restoration of "socialist legality." First, in the balancing of the interests of the state,
the enterprise, and the individual, the last two are now being given
much consideration, at least in official pronouncements. Second,
the rights and responsibilities of the state, enterprises, and individuals are being codified and are henceforth to be enforced through
courts and other well-defined judiciary agencies. Given the regime's dialectical philosophy and the monopolistic power position of
the party (the party is still above the law) it is unlikely that standards will remain fixed once and for all or that arbitrariness will be
totally eliminated. However, the process of defining rights and responsibilities in greater detail than hitherto, even broaching the
touchy question of the judiciary's independence, and the fact that
there are laws and courts to enforce them, would seem to be a positive development from the standpoint of individual workers and
peasants. In particular the right to the household plot and to trade
in village fairs, the removal of the stigma attached in the past to a
person's or his family's incorrect social origin, the rehabilitation
of numerous victims of the Cultural Revolution and the antirightist
campaign of 1957, the promise that there are to be no more cultural
revolutions, and the gradual if somewhat hesitant admission that the
xia xiang* movement was unjust to those involved and to their

---

*Xia xiang refers to the vast campaign to resettle urban edu-
cated youths in the countryside in order to prevent teenage unemployment in the cities. The movement gathered momentum after 1967.

families may be expected to have, on balance, a constructive motivating impact. If justice remains imperfect and subject to shifting standards, at least by comparison with periods of Maoist euphoria, there is now less capriciousness to the decision process. It can be argued, of course, that the increase in socialist legality is purely relative, a question of "who/whom," and that the victims of former persecutions now victimize their erstwhile persecutors. At any rate the tightening up of rules and procedures and the structuring of law enforcement are likely to act as a deterrent to absenteeism, malingering on the job, and other breaches of labor discipline. An incidental, not unimportant, advantage of straightening out the legal mess is that it may reassure foreign lenders and investors. A new commercial code has been prepared; it contains provisions regarding the protection of foreign investments, joint ventures, patent rights, and third-party arbitration.

The third plenary session of the Eleventh Central Committee of the Communist Party of China (December 22, 1978) instructed the State Council to carry out the following policies designed to improve the material well-being of China's peasants. First, the government's quota grain purchase price was to be increased by 20 percent starting in 1979 when the summer grain is marketed. The above quota grain purchase price was to be raised by 50 percent. "Depending on the concrete conditions" purchase prices were also to be raised "step by step" for cotton, oil-bearing and sugar crops, animal byproducts, aquatic and forestry products, and other farm and sideline products. This, in fact, was done in 1979 when procurement prices for 18 farm products (including grain, cotton, and oil-bearing crops) were raised by 24.8 percent on the average. Second, the factory price and the market price of farm machinery, chemical fertilizer, insecticides, plastics, and other manufactured goods for farm use were cut by 10 to 15 percent in 1979 and 1980 "on the basis of reduced cost of production." These two steps were intended to improve agriculture's terms of trade with industry. They are reminiscent of Soviet agricultural reforms of the late 1960s. The hike in the government's agricultural procurement prices is not to be pawned off on the urban consumer. "The market price of all food grain will remain unchanged, and the selling price of other farm products needed for daily life must also be kept stable; if some prices have to be raised, appropriate subsidies will be given to the consumers."[19] In fact, retail prices of eight food items (pork, beef, mutton, poultry, eggs, vegetables, fish, milk) were raised by about 30 percent in November 1979. Farm-related subsidies that are already formidable will rise still higher, at least until such time as farm efficiency improves and average production costs decline. Third, national figures for the state purchase quota for grain and the agricultural tax (paid in kind) are to be based on the five-year quotas 1971-1975 for "a fairly long period to come" (presumably for a minimum of five years), and government grain purchases are never to be "excessive." These measures confirm our suspicion, voiced earlier, regarding the former combination of low procurement prices, high and unpredictable compulsory delivery quotas, and probably exacting and unstable agricultural taxes. The Ministry of Finance early in 1979 introduced several tax reform measures aimed at raising agricultural income by an estimated 1 billion yuan a year. Three major measures were involved: commune processing enterprises with annual net profits of less than 300 yuan were given tax-exempt status (previously income tax applied to annual net profits in excess of 600 yuan); financially troubled new industrial enterprises in rural areas (exclusive of tobacco factories, distilleries, wineries, and cotton mills) have been exempted from taxes for two to three years, while in frontier countries and national autonomous regions the tax holiday period is to be five years; areas with a per capita grain output below the guaranteed minimum level were exempted from paying the agricultural tax.[20]

Egalitarian systems of income distribution in the countryside are being rolled back and work-point accounting, either by piecework or according to the work grade method, is being revived.[21] Stress is put on the necessity for managements to calculate and distribute work points honestly in conformity with the principle "to each according to his work." This necessity becomes the more urgent as the more open, mass democratic methods of supervising the calculation and distribution of work points—methods that involved periodic meetings of all members of a team or production brigade—come to an end.

Innovation

The "red versus expert" contradiction has been resolved for the time being. At the philosophical level it is now explained that, if there is contradiction, it is a benign one of the "among the people" variety to be resolved at the policy level through a united front of all who can be united. "How can you label as 'white' a man who studies hard to improve his knowledge and skills?"[22] He is red who catches mice: "A correct political attitude involves devotion to work. . . . The economy is the goal; politics is only the way that leads to this goal."[23] This viewpoint is articulated more clearly by some leaders (for example, Deng) than by others (for example, Hua). As on other matters of ideology and practice, publicly expressed unanimity on this issue remains shaky. For the time being

at least, intellectuals must again be used for the purpose of modernization. "They are worthy of the title 'red and expert,' fit to be
called our working class's own scientific and technical force."[24]
The poisonous weeds of 1957 and the "stinking ninth" of the Cultural
Revolution have once more become socialism's fragrant flowers
blooming and contending within a new united front.

The educational reform dating back to the Cultural Revolution
has been reversed. "Book learning" and pure research have been
rehabilitated, graduate study has been restored, entrance examina-
tions to colleges and universities based on knowledge and ability
have been reinstituted, curricula are being revised in a direction
opposite from that taken during the reform years, and periods of
study are being lengthened. The worker and peasant propaganda
teams have been expelled from the schools. Large numbers of
Chinese students and teachers are being sent abroad for training.
Special schools for gifted youngsters have been set up. The stress
is on talent, ability, intellectual accomplishment, and rigor.

While worker and peasant innovations and intermediate technology are still mentioned, the emphasis has clearly shifted to not
just modern, but the most up-to-date technology available: "The
crux of the four modernizations is the mastery of modern science
and technology." In the past, foreign observers usually assumed
that China's local, labor-intensive, small and medium industries
did not compete with large, capital-intensive industry for materials,
but used what was available on the spot and would otherwise have
remained unused. This apparently has not been so. Local enterprises, including miniature commune enterprises, competed all
over the country for scarce materials with large enterprises.[25]
From now on, when this happens, the small competitors will be
chopped down.

Planning

The problem here, it will be recalled, has been planlessness
and neglect of the theory of central planning. Both are presently
being attended to. It is clear from the number of planning documents
coming out of Peking that both long-term and yearly plans are again
being formulated. Presumably the planning bureaucracy is being rebuilt. The more interesting and important question is how good are
those plans?

Under Maoist influence the theory of central planning in both
its physical and value aspects had been neglected. The creation of
the Academy of the Social Sciences and of graduate study under the
Academy's auspices, the number of theoretical and policy articles

devoted to questions of macro planning, the rehabilitation of prominent economists who had fallen afoul of the radicals, of economic
journals, and the "law of value," the importance attached to the role
of the People's Bank in financial control over the plan, all this and
more testifies to a renewed interest in questions of the theory and
techniques of central planning. I think that structurally the drift of
the post-Gang reforms has been in the direction of the contemporary
Soviet economy. The natural place for the Chinese to learn the
theory and methodology of administratively inclined macro planning
would be Moscow. I suspect that without admitting it, the Soviet
experience will be an important study source for the Chinese simply
because the Chinese and Soviet economies are brothers under the
skin, structurally not too far apart.

Culturally, however, the Japanese are more understandable
to the Chinese and their record of economic performance since the
end of World War II, especially as regards closing the technological
gap with the United States, has been superior to that of the Soviets.
At this time it is to Japan that China has turned for advice on macro
planning, despite the structural differences in the contemporary
Chinese and Japanese economic systems. The Japan Economic Research Center has been approached by the Chinese about the possibility of assistance in establishing input-output tables and a macro
model for the economy with coal, electric power, oil, petrochemi-
cals, steel, and machine-building as the leading sectors. [26]

Among the theoretical problems to be resolved in Chinese
macro planning are the following: the distribution of decision-
making power on key issues among the center, the economic regions, and the provinces; the distribution of decision-making power
between the party and governmental organs in charge of the plan;
the relative weights to be attached to physical and financial planning,
and—what is not quite the same—to administrative and "economic"
levers; and how to reconcile the gigantic capital expenditures on
heavy (including defense) industry with the declared objective of
keeping agriculture at the top of the planners' scale of preferences
and raising the material welfare of the mass of consumers.

In the midst of Western euphoria about the prospect of a billion
new customers there are a few voices that counsel caution. Saburo
Okita, head of the Japan Economic Research Center and one of the
people behind Japan's post-World War II economic miracle, warns
that the Chinese "want to do everything at once." The London Economist says of Chinese planning: "Think of a number; then double it."

CONCLUSION

It was argued that the changes in China's economy that
we examined in the last section have been made because—

according to the new Chinese leadership under Hua and Deng—they were needed to enable the economy to progress rapidly along a modern, technology-intensive path best represented by the spirit and objectives of the ten-year plans, even in their scaled-down post-1978 version. The institutions that thus far have been discarded or modified were the products of Maoist thought and policy. It was also argued earlier that these Maoist portions of China's economic structure were additions to what in essence was a Soviet-type, administratively inclined, command economy. The additions ranged from complete institutional arrangements to nuances of emphasis. Integrated with the parent body they constituted an interesting and novel variant of the Soviet system. Now these Maoist additions are being dismantled and thus the Chinese economy resembles more than ever its contemporary Soviet counterpart, allowance being made for China's different developmental age and cultural idiosyncracies. The implications of this renewed resemblance are intriguing and of some significance for the choice of direction that China's economic reforms might take.

At this stage, the dismantling of Maoist economic accretions means a return to the status quo ante; to the marginally modified Soviet-type system of the early to mid 1960s, allowing for inevitable but not fundamental changes because of the passage of time. The Chinese macro system of planning, although bureaucratically more decentralized than the contemporary Soviet system, is based on the same general principles of vertical information flows and administrative orders. The relationship between the party and governmental pyramids in the process of plan formulation and plan execution is not very different from that which prevails in the Soviet Union, indeed in any communist country except Yugoslavia. Price and wage setting procedures and the relatively passive role assigned to prices in the process of resource allocation are quite similar, as are the detailed (essentially cost plus) procedures used in price determination. The self-sufficiency of branches of the economy (vertical enterprise or ministry integration) is not a Maoist but a Soviet phenomenon traceable to taut planning and the consequent uncertainties in the supply of inputs. Difficulties encountered in the dissemination of advanced technology through the economy is likewise a Soviet systemic problem rather than the result of sabotage by the Gang of Four. At the micro level the likeness between the Soviet and Chinese systems is equally striking. While the organizational details differ over time, the decision-making powers of enterprise managements on key matters are very similar in both economies: they are, for one thing, quite small and narrowly defined. The relationship between the planners and cooperative agricultural enterprises in both countries consists essentially in the compulsory delivery quota and the (state fixed) quota and above-quota procurement prices. While the rural people's commune may be seen as a Maoist creation, the basic production and income distribution unit in China is the production team, roughly equivalent to an elementary producers' cooperative (lower-level collective farm). Perhaps the most important difference between China's and Soviet Russia's economy is in the way labor is allocated among different employments and geographical areas: administratively in China; mainly through wage differentials in the Soviet Union.

Given the systemic family relationship, chances are that having removed the Maoist barriers to intensive growth, the Chinese will discover that other more intractable obstacles to modernization remain built into the Soviet system. For example, the restoration of the directorial principle, insistence on strict economic accounting, socialist legality, and managerial bonuses (even if linked to profit performance) do not guarantee that enterprises will carry out all major plan norms and that the job will be done efficiently. Profit, profitability rates, sales, and other "synthetic" value indicators will merely produce new distortions in managerial behavior if the prices on which they are based do not approximately express the scarcity relationships in the economy. Reconciling the interests of the state, the enterprise, and the individual participants in the economic process (as consumers and suppliers of labor) will not necessarily be promoted by paying more attention to individual rights and expanding the rights of enterprises. As Soviet experience has shown, improving the material standing of farms and farmers does not (given the system's other hindrances) automatically guarantee an upsurge in labor productivity and output. It could be argued, in fact, that the formalization and routinization of economic behavior, the attempt presently being made to encase all economic activity in administrative boxes subject to innumerable regulations and bureaucratic control, will lessen what flexibility the economy did possess when the Gang was around; that Soviet-type ossification will set in; and "one thousand horses will (again) stand mute."

That is why it is not inconceivable that the reforms may yet go beyond the present "Soviet" system, that they may venture into forbidden areas and explore bolder combinations of administration and market, command and allocative spontaneity. Whether such movement occurs will depend to a considerable extent on the strength of the opposition to the present reform movement—an opposition that is already appalled by the rapidity with which Mao's economic legacy has been abandoned.

NOTES

1. For example, Thomas Rawski, Industrialization, Technology, and Employment in the People's Republic of China (Washington, D.C.: World Bank, Staff Working Papers, August 1978); Shannon R. Brown, "Foreign Technology and Economic Growth," Problems of Communism, July-August 1977, pp. 30-40.

2. Robert F. Dernberger, "The Program for Agricultural Transformation in the People's Republic of China," Proceedings of the Seventh Sino-American Conference on Mainland China (Taipei: Institute of International Relations, 1978), pp. II-2-19. Rawski, op. cit., estimates that labor-intensive activities accounted for about half the increase in the gross value of agricultural output in China between 1952 and 1975. Hu Chiao-mu (Hu Qiaomu) in his important "Observe Economic Laws, Speed Up the Four Modernizations," Peking Review (hereafter PR), No. 46 (November 17, 1978), p. 22 says: "After 1958, wages did not increase regularly, nor did labor productivity; industrial growth had to count entirely or largely on increasing the number of workers and staff. If the yearly 8.7 percent rate of increase in labor productivity [achieved from 1953 through 1957] had remained constant, then labor productivity in industry, capital construction, transport and communications alone would have been three times as high in 1977 as it actually was."

3. Dernberger, op. cit., pp. I-2-23 and II-2-25, and Tables 1 and 2 on pp. II-2-22 and II-2-24. In more recent pronouncements, Chinese spokesmen have admitted the "sluggish" and "slow" growth in farm production and its high degree of labor intensity. See, for example, Hu Chiao-mu, op. cit., p. 18.

4. Workers were told that they were the masters of the workplaces. Now it is said that some evil people had twisted the meaning of this rather unambiguous statement: "If we are all called kung [masters of the common good] then it is not necessary to keep accounts." Ching-chi Yen-chiu (Economic Research), No. 4 (Peking: April 20, 1978), pp. 17-20.

5. In the days of the Gang "it made no difference whether a worker went to work or not; it made no difference how much work he did; it made no difference whether he did his job well or not. . . . In some units workers did nothing the year round but got paid all the same; in other units, all jobs were done by temporary workers while the regular workers goldbricked, did their own thing, or just fooled around." Hu Chiao-mu, op. cit., p. 19.

6. According to Hu Chiao-mu, the average annual progressive increase in total industrial output value during the First Five-Year Plan (1953-1957) was 18 percent; the average annual progressive increase in labor productivity was 8.7 percent; and 7.4 percent for

wages. During that period 59 percent of the industrial expansion was brought about by a growth in labor productivity.

7. Dwight H. Perkins, "Growth and Changing Structure in China's Twentieth Century Economy," in China's Modern Economy in Historical Perspective, ed. Dwight H. Perkins (Stanford, Calif.: Stanford University Press, 1975), p. 153. In 1979-1980 consumer goods prices in China were rising at an annual rate in excess of 10 percent.

8. The practice of contract labor predates the Cultural Revolution. At that earlier time it was also the source of much friction in labor ranks.

9. Hu Chiao-mu, PR, No. 47 (November 24, 1978), pp. 18-20.

10. This is implied by Ching Hua (Ginghua) in "How to Speed Up China's Agricultural Development," PR, No. 42 (October 20, 1978), p. 10.

11. Hu Chiao-mu, November 17, op. cit., p. 18.

12. Liu Pang (Liu Bang), "How to Get High Yields in Agriculture," PR, No. 39 (September 29, 1978), p. 21. Jiansu Province is among the agriculturally more advanced and prosperous. On January 14, 1979, peasants (including a number from Jiangsu) demonstrated in Tiananman square for more food and an end to oppression. "We only have one pound of rice per person per day," said one Jiangsu peasant, "not enough vegetables, and sometimes a little pork," New York Times, January 15, 1979, p. A3.

13. Hen Min, "Reclaiming Wasteland," PR, No. 26 (June 30, 1978), p. 12. The reclamation target is accompanied by sober warnings (which draw on the experience of the Great Leap) about the dangers of "wholesale deterioration of the natural environment."

14. "Minister Apologizes to Peasants," PR, No. 36 (September 8, 1978), p. 21.

15. Estimated 1975 indexes of industrial production in China (1957 = 100): producer goods, 600; machinery, 1,160; consumer goods, 370-380. CIA, China Economic Indicators, October 1977, p. 1.

16. The text may be found in PR, July 20, 1979, pp. 24-26.

17. Hu Chiao-mu, November 17, op. cit., p. 21; PR, No. 41 (October 13, 1978), p. 8; "How Marxists Look at Material Interests," PR, No. 41 (October 13, 1978), p. 8.

18. Renmin Ribao (RR), November 22, 1978, p. 2. Also, RR, June 24, 1978, p. 2; PR, No. 16 (April 21, 1978), pp. 6-8; PR, No. 34 (August 25, 1978), pp. 23-26; PR, No. 38 (September 22, 1978), p. 30. Authors, who are salaried state employees—like musicians and artists—do not receive royalties. However, they are now permitted to receive supplements to their basic salaries based on the number of pages they write. The promulgation of a copyright law is being considered. New York Times, May 8, 1979, p. A3.

19. Communique of the Third Plenary Session of the Eleventh Central Committee of the Communist Party of China, PR, No. 52 (December 29, 1978), p. 13.

20. PR, March 16, 1979, p. 12. In 1977 taxes from rural areas were said to have accounted for only 3.35 percent of the countryside's gross industrial and agricultural output value.

21. The "mass democratic" neoegalitarian rural income distribution systems of Great Leap and Cultural Revolution vintage are described by R. M. Bernardo in his Popular Management and Pay in China (Quezon City: University of Philippines Press, 1977), pp. 13-18. On the piecework and work-grade methods, see J. S. Prybyla, The Chinese Economy: Problems and Policies (Columbia: University of South Carolina Press, 1978), pp. 60-65.

22. Deng Xiaoping Speech to Science Conference (March 18-31, 1978, PR, No. 12 (1978), p. 15.

23. RR, May 5, 1978, pp. 1-4, Guangming Ribao (GR), May 22, 1978, p. 1.

24. Deng Xiaoping, op. cit., p. 14.

25. From 1974 through 1978 a single county sent out 5,000 persons on materials buying missions for its small enterprises. The buyers (the equivalent of Soviet "fixers" or tolkachi) visited 28 provinces and municipalities. RR, May 29, 1978, p. 2.

26. New York Times, January 9, 1979, p. D3.

3
SOCIALIST MODERNIZATION: THE HUNGARIAN ALTERNATIVE IN THEORY AND PRACTICE

WHY IS THE HUNGARIAN MODEL OF INTEREST ?

The post-Stalin political "thaw" in the Soviet Union of the mid-to late 1950s was accompanied by much talk (until then unheard) about the right of different countries to pick their own "path to socialism." The Polish and Hungarian events of 1956 made it plain that the old Stalinist model of the command economy with its autarkic prescriptions was not right for the small countries of Eastern Europe, given their narrow resource bases and limited domestic markets. Apart from that, the model needed to be changed to promote the modernization of the socialist economic structure.

The "different paths to socialism" doctrine was subject to specific, if not always well-articulated, restrictions. Externally, any chosen path had to be acceptable to the Soviet Union. Since the Soviet reforms of the Stalinist model turned out to have been very conservative, stopping well short of significant systemic alterations, the limits set on socialist experimentation elsewhere became quite restrictive in actual implementation (theoretical discussion of various hypothetical models was, by comparison, bold). Thus, the implementation of the Czech blueprint for market socialism, which, among other offenses, contained a proposal for the reorganization of enterprises in a Yugoslav workers' councils direction, was halted by the deployment of Soviet armor in 1968. The opportunity to give the Yugoslavs a dose of the same medicine had been missed much earlier, and nothing tangible could be done about the Yugoslav heresy at this late stage. Intervention has to await the death of Tito. Beginning in 1958, the Chinese went their own leftist way. Soviet attempts to teach them a lesson by withdrawing technical assistance and clamping down on credits signally failed to achieve the intended purpose. So China, too, followed its own socialist path, but in a direction opposite from Yugoslavia's.

Domestically, Marxist-Leninist socialism, even in its post-Stalin reincarnation, had to conform to two basic conditions: first, continued power monopoly wielded by the Communist Party; second, comprehensive (not necessarily total) socialization of the means of production. Economically, the power monopoly of the Communist Party meant, and still means, the exercise of central authority by the communists over key macroeconomic variables. These include the setting of limits on the width and depth of systemic reforms, the structure of income distribution, allocation of resources to public and private uses (including the overall pattern of investment), the level of employment and the price level, and foreign economic relations. In no case is this power altogether surrendered to lower-echelon authorities or shared with competing political parties. Not even in Yugoslavia, where the path that the national economy takes is theoretically determined by a market aggregation of enterprise and commune plans, does the monoparty through its central state machine give up its prerogative to prod the economy in directions it considers appropriate. Moreover, the central state reserves the right to intervene directly at the level of micro detail whenever it decides that its macro objectives are threatened by what it considers "perverse" action on the part of the economy's micro units. Comprehensive socialization means that the strategically important sectors, subsectors, and industries remain in the hands of the state; but not necessarily all sectors, subsectors, industries, or enterprises. Outright state ownership of this kind is considered both ideologically desirable and economically helpful to the center's implementation of aggregate economic policy. Within such comprehensive state ownership, the extent of microeconomic rights exercised by individual economic units (for example, state and cooperative enterprises) can vary considerably, from narrow (Soviet Union) to very wide (Yugoslavia).

If the contemporary Soviet-type economy is taken as standard, then the contemporary Hungarian-type economy is mildly revisionist to the "right." It goes farther than the Soviet system in diffusing goal-setting power and in introducing market-related forces into its information coordination and incentive mechanisms. It goes much farther than the reformed Soviet system in removing the planning center from microscopic intervention in enterprise affairs and in shifting from physical to market-related value-type indicators. The distance actually traveled away from Stalinist administrative command toward market socialism is, however, much shorter than that which had earlier been covered by reformist thought. As we shall see, the limits placed in Hungary on the actual remodeling of the old Stalinist growth engine (1948-1956) were partly internal, partly imposed by the presence of the Soviet Union and the Soviet Union's more conservative East European partners. In the event, the Hungarian model has not been adopted by any other East European country and the Hungarians themselves have been compelled since 1972 to pull in the reins and align themselves more with the Soviet sphere's relatively innocuous reforms. If this is so, what, it may be asked, is the importance of the Hungarian new economic mechanism (NEM)?

At the practical, operational plane the interest of the Hungarian solution rests in the following:

An important objective of the reform was economic modernization. The need was to raise factor efficiency, stimulate innovation, lower the material intensity of production, and cure the balance-of-payments disequilibria of an essentially transforming economy—small, poor in natural resources, with an almost stationary labor force. At the time the reforms were implemented (1968) Hungary was experiencing rising incremental capital/output ratios, sluggish increases of labor productivity, and deteriorating terms of trade. The quality of Hungary's export goods was, by and large, not good enough to find ready buyers in capitalist markets; such goods had to be sold, therefore, to other socialist customers who had little say in the matter. Most of the other problems that confront centrally planned Soviet-type command economies were present in Hungary, perhaps more starkly than elsewhere. The behavioral characteristics generated among planners, enterprise managers, workers, and consumers by the administrative command economy were there: among them the willfulness of centralized power, risk avoidance, short-range horizons, precautionary hoarding, underemployment in the midst of a labor shortage, absenteeism, black marketeering, and user frustrations.

> We proceeded by learning from our own mistakes,
> from the damage done by ourselves. We already know
> that what we plan never gets exactly realized. . . .
> Our technical level is lagging behind many countries,
> and we do not use every possibility to make up for our
> backwardness. . . . A plan comprising every detail
> is inconceivable. . . . It follows that highly central-
> ized, highly detailed planning cannot be justified even
> in principle. [1]

The need to go beyond mere tinkering with the old system, to tackle basic systemic reforms, was felt by all strata of Hungarian society. The impulse to reform was not the result of an intraparty coup or of a shift in ideological perception. The reform (especially the theoretical side of it) had the support of the Communist Party apparatus. Because it was conducted with due deference to the sensibilities of the Soviet Union and did not broach sensitive subjects that lie beyond the pale of Soviet ideological tolerance (for example, workers' councils, competing political formations— which is what the Czechs aired in the heady spring of 1968), it encountered patronizing neglect, if not enthusiastic support, in Moscow. Casting the key issues of the debate in mathematical, highly abstract terms helped to keep Soviet vigilance at bay.

Modernization was at all times contingent on three constraints elevated by the leadership to the rank of national goals: control of inflation, avoidance of unemployment, and improvement of living standards. The first two were to conflict in the course of the reform with the objective of improving dynamic efficiency. An additional constraint, as it turned out, was the leadership's unwillingness to tamper with the existing industrial structure, which was marked by a high degree of concentration. This constraint, too, tended to hamper the attempt to improve efficiency through stimulating market competition.[2] These various constraints (especially those concerning employment, inflation, and the standard of living) are shared by other socialist societies seeking models of economic modernization. Indeed, full employment and price stability are among the most vaunted achievements of socialism, even though, as we have seen, they usually conceal underemployment and suppressed inflation. The Hungarian model is, therefore, politically acceptable to other socialist countries insofar as domestic economic goals are concerned.

Analysis of the results of the reform (around 1975) showed that the three major constraints were not violated. Improvement in living standards did take place without overt inflation or unemployment, and the structure of industry was not altered. Labor productivity in industry rose at an average annual rate of 4.7 percent a year over the period 1968-1975 (compared with 5.2 percent a year over the period 1961-1967 and 6.1 percent a year over 1971-1975). Average yields of the major crops increased during the reform period as did yields of milk and eggs. Per capita consumption of high protein foods (meat, fish, dairy products) rose significantly (for example, per capita meat and fish consumption in 1965 was 53.2 kilograms; in 1975, 70-71 kilograms). Per capita real income from 1968 through 1975 rose at an annual average rate of 5.3 percent (compared with 4 percent a year from 1961 through

1967 and 4.6 percent a year from 1971 through 1975). Real dis-
posable income per capita rose at an average annual rate of 5.4
percent in the period 1971-1975 compared with 8 percent a year in
1966-1970 and 4.6 percent a year in 1961-1975. The average annual rate of increase in the consumer price index over the reform
period 1968-1975 was 2 percent compared with 0.5 percent per
year over 1961-1967 and 2.8 percent per year over 1971-1975. A
good part of the post-1973 increase was due to rising import costs.
There was serious deterioration in the dollar balance of trade
(trade with Western countries): the average annual balance on the
dollar account over the period 1968-1975 was $-109.7 million
(compared with an annual average of $-8.7 million over 1961-1967
and $-182.1 million a year from 1971 through 1975). By the end
of 1975 Hungary's net hard currency debt stood at $2 billion, most
of it owed to Western commercial banks. The record on innovation
was mixed: the rate of introduction of new products increased, but
there were lags in discontinuing the production of obsolescent goods
and in introducing new goods. Moreover, most of the innovation
that was actually achieved was centrally sponsored, that is, it came
from above, like in the old days, rather than from the enterprises.
Stock building was reduced and the supply of materials and spare
parts was marginally improved. However, the ratio of unfinished
investment projects persisted and, in fact, somewhat deteriorated
compared with prereform years.[3] All in all, the record seems to
have been better as regards employment, price stability, and real
income than with respect to dynamic efficiency. The modernization
picture is at best clouded. Proponents of the reform would argue
that this is so because the brakes on the new economic mechanism
inherited from the old system were never fully removed; indeed,
they were strengthened after 1972. In the circumstances, the new
mechanism never quite got a chance to show what it could do.
However, the record remains mixed and the future of the experiment is in doubt, largely because of international developments
over which the Hungarians have no control.

Theoretically, the Hungarian reforms are of absorbing interest. They constitute a blueprint for systemic changes that result
in a mixture of central planning and something approaching market
decentralization. They represent an innovative and sophisticated
attempt to introduce a guided market economy and wean the system
away from the old Soviet-type administrative prototype.

GOAL-SETTING

Conceptually one of the pillars of the Hungarian reform is
economic decentralization, which means two things: the central

authorities retain control over key economic variables, the "main directions and proportions of the economy"; and detailed microeconomic targets for individual enterprises, as well as enterprise "control by the forint," are abolished.[4] The authorities retain control through the government's macroeconomic policy that employs economic instruments such as taxes, subsidies, agricultural purchase prices, and bank credits to channel activity into the desired grooves, or stimulate or dampen it. The centrally formulated goals are primarily indicative, not mandatory. They are given concrete expression in the state's long-term central investment programs. In other words, economic units in the economy are guided by state fiscal and monetary action toward the general goals desired by the state.

The microeconomic targets are replaced by the formulation of output level and assortment targets by the enterprises themselves, based on commercial contracts concluded with other firms (or in the case of collective farms, with the state purchasing agencies) in pursuit of profit and in response to user demand, costs, and price signals. Unlike the contemporary Soviet-type economy in which contracts between enterprises are based on centrally predetermined material balances, in principle the contractual relations of Hungarian enterprises are lateral, freely entered into; the balances of the economy emerge from these contracts, rather than the other way around.

Goal-setting in the Hungarian economy is based on the concept of the "visible hand": the manipulation by the state of managerial behavior through "legitimate" instruments of economic policy (that is, not through direct physical input allocations and administratively determined output orders). The model makes provision for restrained spontaneity:

> in order to control development in line with a plan, it is not necessary to influence every event, action or process of the economy, but only those which involve anything beyond the simple repetition of what happened so far. . . . An engine factory needs no instructions for producing engines and not shoes, nor should we instruct a shoe factory to produce shoes. They know best which category of consumers they should be aiming at to satisfy, and also, what material means and labor are necessary for this purpose.[5]

INFORMATION-COORDINATION MECHANISM

Beginning with a Soviet-type command economy, the vesting in enterprises of broader decision-making rights would still add up only to administrative decentralization unless the information system on which such decisions are based and the economy's coordination mechanism are substantively changed. Specifically, the former system of physical input allocations and output commands addressed to enterprises and the system of nonscarcity prices have to be thoroughly transformed. Telling enterprises to follow the profit criterion, as the Russians have done, does not alter things much because "profits . . . cannot correctly measure the quality of the work of the enterprise unless there are correct price relations." In Hungary it was "only after long discussions [that] the idea [could] be developed that correct price relations should, on the whole, correspond to the socially necessary input proportions under given conditions, with modifications considering demand and supply, that is, market conditions."[6] The price system had to communicate information to the enterprise decision makers on relative resource costs and utilities within the system. Such information tends to be the less accurate the more imperfect the market within which the prices are formed.

The Hungarians approached the problem in several steps. First, the old centrally set industrial wholesale prices were revised so as to make them more closely aligned with average branch production costs. Agricultural procurement prices were raised. These were essentially standard Soviet-type reforms. They involved the revaluation of fixed assets, introduction of higher depreciation charges and of a charge on capital (which, however, did not reflect the opportunity cost of capital), establishment of differential rent for some natural resources in the form of a graduated land tax, and the calculation of profitability in relation to total assets rather than production costs (the Soviets also moved, albeit partially, in that direction).[7]

Second, as already noted, physical input allocations, output targets, and other production-related centrally formulated indicators to enterprises were—with few exceptions—done away with. This included the removal of compulsory delivery quotas for collective farms. Guided by the profit objective, enterprises were expected to get all the information they needed from the new price system.

Prices

This system consisted of four categories of prices: fixed, maximum, limit, and free. Fixed prices covered basic materials, state grain procurements, fuels, and indispensable consumption goods. They were centrally determined and changed. Being basic and pervasive in their influence, they represented a significant constraint on the extent to which the system could be marketized, and consequently on the reliability of the information mechanism. Maximum prices meant that for some commodities the center established upper limits that could legally be charged. However, the seller could, if he so wished, charge less than the maximum. In the case of limit prices, both the permissible maxima and minima were fixed by the center. However, within those limits, sellers were free to charge whatever price they saw fit. Finally, free prices were determined by supply and demand forces in the marketplace without any legal or administrative restraint. This category covered a wide variety of consumption items as well as a range of semifabricates. The new system was an improvement over its predecessor mainly because it relieved the center of the chore of fixing, supervising, and changing a multitude of prices, most of them relating to fairly minor items. By this token, the grosser irrationalities and resultant bottlenecks connected with Soviet-type pricing were eliminated. On the other hand, because of the continued presence of centrally fixed prices for key materials and consumption necessities, the new system could not function reliably as an information-gathering and processing device that would signal to producers and users intelligence on the utilities and comparative costs of scarce resources.

Institutionally, the continued presence of price controls in strategic areas—one of the so-called transitional brakes on the reform—constituted a holdover from the old command system and a constant threat to decentralization. The maintenance of price controls was no doubt politically necessary. The removal of such controls would have inflated the prices of consumer necessities dramatically, with possibly equally dramatic political consequences. The government did eventually raise the retail prices of some key (highly subsidized) consumer commodities, but this was done after careful assessment of what the political climate could bear, given the money illusion created among consumers by a long-standing policy of keeping the prices of necessities well below their clearing levels.

That is one reason why the original long-term objective of the reformers to move gradually toward ever greater decontrol and rising importance of the "free" price category did not materialize. After 1973 the threat of imported inflation made such progressive decontrol even less likely. In 1968, when the reform was introduced, 23 percent of total turnover was subject to free prices. It was expected that by 1975 the proportion would rise to 50 percent. In fact, in 1975 free prices accounted for at most 38 percent of turnover. This figure exaggerates the actual importance of free prices because of the increasing pressure put on such prices by various governmental regulations that defined cost procedures to be used to determine "free" prices and laid down guidelines for distinguishing between "fair" and "unfair" profit margins.[8]

Domestic Competition

Another reason for the modest distance traveled by the marketization reform, compared with original intentions, was the unwillingness of the authorities to alter the existing industrial structure. Ever since 1963, when a consolidation of Hungarian industry was carried out, the industrial sector has been highly concentrated. About 800 state enterprises produce more than 90 percent of the industrial output. Half of these firms employ more than 5,000 workers.[9] The enterprises are directly under branch ministries, and their managers are appointed and removed by these ministries. In such conditions there is not likely to be much market competition, and price formation—however "free"—inevitably becomes an exercise in oligopoly. In turn, oligopolistic price determination tends to increase the likelihood of central state intervention in the pricing process, so that before long the original impulse to marketize the economy is smothered under a mass of administrative regulations, each giving rise to a whole brood of picky administrative details.

The Hungarian attempt to transform prices from centrally determined cost-plus backup instruments of physical planning to opportunity cost indicators, and coordinators of production and consumption decisions, was also frustrated by the socialist belief in the immortality of enterprises. For market prices to perform their information-coordination job, there must be at least a modicum of price competition in the market. When, as was the case in Hungary, unprofitable firms are kept afloat by subsidies and when (for various politically understandable reasons) foreign competition is moderated in or excluded from the domestic market, the objective of modernization through marketization is bound to suffer.

On other fronts competitive forces were encouraged, at least initially. Collective farms, for example, were given free reign to decide what to produce, where to buy their inputs, and how much and where to market.[10] This was known as the "multichannel distribution system." It included the establishment of federations of cooperatives that were intended to counterbalance the power of state agencies (especially the procurement agencies). Former restrictions on private subsidiary activities of collective farm households and the collective farms themselves were lifted, and free markets for farm produce and artisan-type products were exempted from the

kind of administrative and legal harassment to which they had often
been subjected in the past. In fact, collective farms were urged to
diversify into nonfarm lines of work such as construction, automo-
tive repairs, restaurant ownership, and so on. [11] As a result, side
by side with a controlled oligopolistic state industrial sector, there
came into being a competitive-to-imperfectly-competitive cluster
of markets dealing in farm produce, repair work, various kinds of
consumer-oriented manufactures and services, residential construction catering, and other activities, including a fair share of moonlighting. For a while the sellers in these markets did quite well;
their real incomes rose more rapidly than those of blue-collar
workers in state industry. Given the pent-up demand for what under
the old system was regarded as "peripheral" activity (that is, provision of consumer goods and services, other than rock-bottom
necessities, and of residential housing), profits reaped in these
markets soon became the targets of ideological criticism. The
familiar charges of "profiteering," "petty bourgeois mentality,"
and "materialism" were heard again and administrative swords
were unsheathed.

An intangible factor, one more difficult to measure, which
inhibited the development of market leadership and coordination in
the post-1968 period, was the behavioral conditioning of managers
as well as many workers carried over from the old administrative
command economy. Whatever the inconveniences of the command
system, it does breed certain behavioral traits that are at once
comfortable to those who exhibit them and difficult to leave behind.
A competitive market setting is not the easiest and calmest environment to operate in. The command system demands of its managers
qualities that in some respects are different from those required
by the competitive market: primarily routine execution of orders
from above and avoidance of risk. The command system supplies
the manager not only with inputs (however insufficient he may judge
them) but with customers as well. It shields the firm from bank-
ruptcy and the workers from unemployment. Shortages of many
consumer goods and services are to a degree made up by a comparatively relaxed pace of work due in large measure to overstaff-
ing. The phenomenon of flight from choice is common among many
managers and some of the more coddled workers in administrative
command systems. Competition and the discipline of the market
are always good when they visit one's competitor; when they strike
close to home, the talk is of equity and the clamor is for protection.
The problem becomes more acute when the reform stops halfway.
Then, in addition to the old rules of the game, one has to learn new
ones; and it is not always clear which set of rules applies in what
particular circumstances.

INCENTIVE MECHANISM

Hungarian reforms of the incentive mechanism (both incentives to managers and workers) are instructive for many reasons, one of which is the conflict that developed quite early on between the imperatives of allocative and dynamic efficiency and what the losers in the adjustment regarded as violations of socialist principles of equity in the distribution of income.

Managerial Incentives

Taking the Stalinist economy as a point of departure, "right" inclined reform of the incentive system may proceed in two steps:

The old unidimensional success indicators (a multitude of them, but in practice usually one: the gross value of output) are replaced by "partial synthetic indicators," for example, sales volume, reduction in materials intensity, increases in labor productivity, profitability, profit, and so on.[12] The synthesis is partial because the step is taken within a context of average cost-plus prices that do not reflect the scarcity relationships of the system.
The various partial synthetic indicators are replaced by a single "synthetic" indicator: profit. This indicator is only as "synthetic" as are the prices from which it emerges. In other words, the shift to profit as the only enterprise success norm requires a prior marketization of the information mechanism.

Soviet reforms never went beyond the first step, and by all accounts there has been regression since. The Hungarian reform moved straightaway to the second step but with only a partial reform of the price (including wage) system. Friss, an economist and a former member of the Hungarian planning hierarchy, asserts:

> Today, state interference in the field of price development does, in general, not serve the purpose at which we aimed when the reformed price system was introduced, namely, that prices should provide correct orientation, i.e., they should fundamentally reflect the socially necessary input proportions. . . . On January 1, 1968 there was no possibility for introducing either a price system reflecting input proportions, or free prices developing according to market relations. The changes that ought to have been made or permitted, were all too great: they would have necessitated, apart

from a radical transformation of the whole price system, an entirely overhauled wage system too, or alternatively, market forces ought to have been allowed to
bring about such an upheaval.[13]

The political costs of the upheaval were realistically regarded as
intolerable. However, in a textbook sense it is also true that if
there are no markets and price incentives, there must be a lot of
detailed directives. If the directives are reduced without being replaced by tolerably competitive markets and prices, things will just
possibly become worse than they were before.

Enterprise Funds

   With profit as the indicator for both industrial and farm enterprises, a system of enterprise profit-based funds was established
through a complex tax structure. Gross enterprise profits were
divided into two parts: the first transferable by the tax to the state
budget, the second retained by the enterprise. The retained part
was divided into three funds, the proportion of net profit going into
each being determined by the tax. The funds were designed for
reserve purposes, "sharing" (that is, payment of managerial and
worker bonuses and communal consumption expenditures), and
"development" (that is, decentralized enterprise investments). In
addition to a portion of profits, the enterprise development fund
was to be fed by depreciation funds and borrowings from the banking
system. Despite high marginal rates of taxation, the size of both
the sharing and the development funds varied directly with enterprise total profits. Bonuses paid to managers (and to a lesser extent to production workers) from the sharing fund also varied
directly with total profits. The reform did not prescribe the proportions of net profits to be allocated to collective farm reserve,
sharing, and development funds. It was merely noted that the
ratios should be compatible with socialist principles of income
distribution.
   The size of the sharing fund (source of managerial bonuses)
was determined by a common formula applied to all enterprises.
This division was different from the Soviet reform that applied
different formulas to different firms. Problems soon cropped up.
A single standard would, of course, have made sense had the price
system not been distorted by the presence of many fixed, maximum,
and limit prices, as well as numerous and very sizable subsidies.
Subsidies, highly differentiated by products and enterprises, represented nearly 55 percent of state enterprise profits in 1972. In

these circumstances profitability (hence the size of managerial bonuses) varied widely among enterprises. In addition, managerial bonuses related to profit were reportedly in some instances 20 times larger than those of production workers. Because of the system of central control over enterprise wages (to be discussed) the size of the bonus distribution to managers varied inversely with the average wage of production workers.[14] Workers in the less "profitable" large state enterprises lost ground, not just relative to managers, but compared with the real incomes of workers in the more "profitable" enterprises, collective farmers' earnings, and the incomes of various self-employed persons engaged in the provision of consumer services. It was thus primarily because of political pressures put on the leadership by blue-collar workers in state industry in the name of distributional equity that all kinds of new brakes on the reform were introduced beginning in the latter part of 1969. "Unjustified profits" were more narrowly defined, the price control power of various planning bodies was strengthened, production workers' wages in the state sector were raised from state budgetary sources, some half-dozen large state enterprises were reorganized, and their "profitability" was improved by direct state administrative and financial intervention. Limits were placed on real estate dealings, moonlighting, decentralized enterprise investments, and the subsidiary nonfarm-related activities of collective farms.

The development fund was intended to serve as a source of decentralized investment. As noted earlier, the fund's monies were to come from a portion of enterprise profit, depreciation allowances, and bank credits. The liberalization of investment decisions led to a sharp increase in enterprise investments, shortages of construction materials, and upward pressure on prices. The decentralized investment was poorly conceived and coordinated in a resource-taut environment. Enterprises were not allowed to suffer the consequences of erroneous decisions taken on the basis of imperfect information but, in line with the immortality principle, were bailed out by state grants. The authorities quickly tightened control over enterprise investments primarily through reduction in bank credits. The figures frequently cited for the proportion of decentralized (enterprise) investment in total investment outlays—roughly 50 percent—is somewhat misleading because it does not show how much autonomy enterprises are left with in this regard. Through the manipulation of bank credit and taxes on enterprise revenues, as well as by informal means of suasion, the central authorities exercise considerable control over the nature, volume, and direction of decentralized investment.

Incentives to Workers

Workers, as we have seen, receive cash bonuses from the sharing fund, but the portion of total worker income represented by such profit-related bonuses is smaller than the portion of total managerial salaries represented by bonuses. The underlying idea is to tie the individual self-interest of managers and workers to the interests of the enterprise as revealed by profit performance, and to link the interests of the enterprise to those of society that, again, are signaled by the "synthetic" profit indicator.

Under the new economic mechanism the center continues to determine basic wage rates for different kinds of jobs. However, it no longer sets the enterprise wages funds, as it used to in the past. Instead it employs "average wage control" as an antiinflationary device. Any increases in average enterprise wages above a certain specified norm (say, 3 percent of the 1967 average wage) provoke a sharp increase in the enterprise's tax liability, the tax being drawn out of the sharing fund before any payment of bonuses. The intent is to discourage the enterprises from bidding up wages in a tight labor market and by such action contributing to cost-push inflation. The actual result has been a tendency for enterprises to hire new workers at wages below the enterprise average and to raise the wages of the already employed workers. In this way bonuses could be distributed without incurring the tax penalty. By and large, however, the average wage control mechanism was successful in controlling wage inflation; the rate of increase of money wages did not exceed the rate of increase in labor productivity. Such inflationary pressures as did occur were due to a combination of increases in the prices of imports and—domestically—to poor coordination and misallocation of investment. Nevertheless, it remains true that progress toward marketization of the economy was hesitant at best: "even in the most liberal reform, the enterprise does not have the freedom to hire workers it considers necessary, and pay them what it believes they are worth in the light of their contributions to sales and profit."[15] By 1976 even these moderately decentralizing measures with respect to wages had been rolled back. Thenceforth the state controlled not only the average wage but began again to regulate enterprise wages in detail.

FOREIGN TRADE

To take advantage of the specialization of labor and benefit from economies of scale, a small country, poor in natural resources and confined to a very limited domestic market, must trade with the world outside. The Stalinist command system, imposed on the countries of Eastern Europe after World War II, treated foreign trade as a sideline activity, subsidiary to self-reliance. East European trade was redirected from the West toward the Soviet Union, and it was carried on for the most part by means of bilateral agreements.

Even in its reformed garb, the Soviet-type economy has two built-in problems with respect to foreign trade. First, internal and external prices are separated by unrealistic exchange rates; second, the domestic seller or buyer is separated from the foreign customer or seller by the state's foreign trade corporations. The insulation of domestic from world prices makes it difficult to make decisions on imports and exports based on meaningful criteria of comparative advantage. It also protects domestic industry from outside competition with unfortunate results on the efficiency of domestic enterprises. The interposition of bureaucrats between domestic users or sellers and foreign sellers and buyers reduces the effectiveness of foreign trade. One would think that the final user is best placed to make decisions regarding the kind of imports that would suit him and his clients best. Similarly, problems are bound to arise when exporters are separated from their customers by the hierarchically superior bureaucracy of the foreign trade corporation and are neither rewarded nor hurt financially if the product they deliver does not exactly fit the customers' needs or conform to their specifications. The domestic producer working for the export market responds under this system to essentially domestic stimuli, originating in the state trading apparatus, rather than to external market signals.

In contrast to the Soviet reform's timid experimentation with administrative means of linking domestic to world economies (decentralization of the foreign trade ministry, calculation of coefficients of foreign trade effectiveness by personnel of the foreign trade corporations), Hungarian reformers spoke of the need to establish an organic (that is, systemic) connection between domestic and foreign markets. Price and cost developments in the outside world (the world of the developed market-oriented countries) were now to have a greater impact on domestic costs and prices. Foreign trade was to "originate stimulating competition in respect of prices, quality, or choice, prompting thereby the domestic productive and trading enterprises to better performance."[16] This organic connection was to be moderated by the state's intervention in behalf of high-cost, but nationally important, enterprises. There was justifiable apprehension that if the windows were suddenly opened to the winds of foreign competition, the blast would likely knock out most of Hungary's oligopolistic state enterprises. The state was therefore to intervene, where appropriate, by means of subsidies, tariffs, licensing arrangements, credit guarantees, and so on. In the event, these theoretically temporary, transitional, and marginal protectionist measures proved very hardy, long lasting, and central.

Conceptually, the two major barriers were removed by the introduction of separate uniform dollar and ruble exchange rates, and the granting to enterprises of the right to trade either directly with foreigners or through the state's foreign trade corporations, the latter acting as commission agents for the enterprises. Thus, at least at the level of theory, an organic relationship was established between domestic and foreign prices and between domestic and foreign exporters and importers. At the policy level the situation was different. Most exporting enterprises continued to be subsidized; some very heavily. The subsidy structure became differentiated by several industry groups. Within each group the marginal firm received enough subsidy to keep it alive, while lower-cost producers in the group reaped differential advantages in the form of higher profit rates. The rate of subsidy was fixed for five years in advance, the aim being not to penalize through sudden subsidy reductions those producers who reduced their costs through technical improvements.[17] In addition to subsidies, a great array of direct and indirect interventionist weapons was soon assembled, and decisions regarding exports and imports are now mostly made by the center on the basis of qualitatively indifferent comparative-cost information. Inflation in dollar markets and the unwillingness of Hungary's East European and Soviet trading partners to transact business otherwise than through state trading corporation channels and largely by means of bilateral agreements have made implementation of the original reformist blueprint extremely problematical. This much can, however, be said: The former complete insulation of foreign and domestic markets has been attenuated and the domestic price structure is marginally more responsive than it used to be to world price trends.[18]

CONCLUSION

The Hungarian-style reform of the original Soviet-type economy was more ambitious and logical in theory than in actual implementation.[19] External constraints and internal pressures, both political and economic, joined to prevent the concept from being fully translated into reality. The blueprint envisaged far-reaching systemic change. In actuality the changes were partial and more superficial. The Hungarian economy remains a species of the

Soviet-type economic genus with, however, some interesting structural mutations.

Because of the partial application of the proposed reforms, the record of achievement remains unclear. Progress toward the sociopolitical objectives of the leadership (full employment, a stable price level, and rising living standards) has been more visible and more readily documented than movement toward the reformers' objective of modernization. Increased efficiency was brought about largely by a better use of formerly idle reserves (reduction in inventory accumulations and the mobilization of underemployed labor for the provision of consumer services on a private or semiprivate basis).

Above all, the Hungarian experience shows how difficult it is to bring about systemic reform, once a centralized administrative command mechanism has been established.

NOTES

1. I. Friss, "Planning and Economic Reform in Hungary," in Progress and Planning in Industry: Proceedings of the International Conference on Industrial Economics, April 1970, ed. Z. Roman (Budapest: Akádemiai Kiadó, 1972), pp. 61-64.
2. The property structure of agriculture, dominated by state and collective farms, was not changed by the reform, although some of the former restrictions on private plot activity were lifted.
3. Richard Portes, "Hungary: Economic Performance, Policy, and Prospects," in East European Economies Post-Helsinki, A Compendium of Papers Submitted to the Joint Economic Committee, Congress of the United States (Washington, D.C.: U.S. Government Printing Office, 1977), pp. 803, 805, 806, 809, and 813. Z. Edward O'Relley, "Hungarian Agricultural Performance and Policy During the NEM," in ibid., pp. 377-78.
4. "Control by the forint" (or ruble, or whatever) is a basic control means of Soviet-type economies. It is the detailed transactions control of an enterprise by the central bank. Every enterprise in the system has an account with the bank and all transactions made by the enterprise in the course of plan fulfillment must be made through book transfers at the bank. The bank is thus in a position to monitor the enterprise's adherence to plan instructions on an on-going basis.
5. Friss, op. cit., pp. 67-68.
6. Ibid., p. 67.
7. Collective farm debts in excess of the value of the revalued fixed assets were written off on December 31, 1966, in line with the policy of easing the financial burdens of agriculture.

8. Morris Bornstein, "Economic Reform in Eastern Europe," in <u>East European Economies Post-Helsinki</u>, op. cit., p. 121.

9. J. S. Prybyla, "Oligipole et Reforme Economique: Le Cas Hongrois," <u>Revue de l'Est</u> 5, no. 3 (July 1974): 115-31. Compare Timothy Hannan, "Lack of Competition: Where It's Found and How Much It Costs," <u>Business Review</u>, Federal Reserve Bank of Philadelphia, May-June 1979, pp. 5-11.

10. This freedom was not extended to the slaughter of cows and hogs, bread grains, tobacco, and some other products designated as state monopoly.

11. Alec Nove, <u>The Soviet Economic System</u> (London: George Allen and Unwin, 1977), p. 292. In the mid-1970s the tax rates on collective farm ancillary activities unrelated to farming were raised, while tax rates on activities closely related to farming were lowered.

12. Friss, op. cit., p. 69.

13. Ibid.

14. Portes, op. cit., p. 785.

15. Bornstein, op. cit., p. 117.

16. Friss, op. cit., p. 70.

17. Egon Neuberger and William Duffy, <u>Comparative Economic Systems: A Decision-Making Approach</u> (Boston: Allyn and Bacon, 1976), p. 298.

18. Prices within Comecon trade follow world prices on a five-year moving average and thus affect the internal price structures of Comecon members.

19. There was much optimism in the early years of the reform. Economic liberalization was, in the opinion of some—although in not so many words—expected to lead to broader freedoms: "Maybe the [marketized] activities in question amount only to a quarter or less of all activities, but they constitute a decisive part, because <u>this</u> is the part which may—in the course of one, two or three five-year periods—gradually <u>restructure</u> the economy and radically transform even those areas of society which go far beyond the economy." Friss, op. cit., p. 68.

4
WORKER PARTICIPATION IN MANAGEMENT: THEORY AND YUGOSLAV PRACTICE

It will be recalled that one of the subjective attributes of economic modernization is participation: the presence of institutional means designed to associate people in the shaping of their social (and, more narrowly, working) environment. In the past the issue of participation had been skirted by all economic systems. It was redefined as a question of finding the right sort of incentive mechanism, one that through an appropriate wage structure would associate the interests of the individual workers with enterprise interests. Strictly speaking, such redefinition does not address itself directly to what is, after all, the essential element of participation, namely democratic governance. Under even the most harmonious wage-cum-profit-sharing system, the organization of enterprises remains hierarchic and dirigiste.

More recently, broadening the base of participation—associating those people directly affected by the choice of objectives and the allocation of resources to the chosen objectives—has become a matter of urgent concern in many market-oriented and administration-oriented systems: from West Germany, where the answer has been worker representation on the supervisory boards of firms, to Communist China, where the solution under the regime of Mao Zedong took the form of the so-called three-in-one combinations at the enterprise level, the putting up of big-character posters by workers, and other means. Broader participation, or "codetermination" as it is sometimes called (joint problem solving), requires the restructuring of existing hierarchic institutions in the direction of a less unequal sharing of power. It is, therefore, likely to meet with opposition and delaying tactics from those presently at the helm: The corporate technostructure in market-oriented economies; the state bureaucracy in administratively oriented systems. The resistance will normally be put up in the name of efficiency; too many cooks, it is argued, spoil the broth, or as the Chinese phrase it: "where there are too many hens, there are no eggs; where there are too many people, there is disorder." Despite such warnings, the problem will not go away. It will not be solved simply by paying people more, even though some studies show that the rush toward mass consumption (the drive to earn) seems to be gaining on the drive to participate. Proponents of participation by workers in the management of their workplaces are also aware of the possible conflict between self-determination and economic performance; between industrial democracy and economic return. They do not see this as an absolute contradiction, an inverse relationship; rather they regard it as a question of finding the right organizational form of participation and the correct amount of input by the rank and file into the decision-making process.

The most comprehensive theoretical formulation of worker participation (or labor management) is Jaroslav Vanek's The General Theory of Labor-Managed Market Economies and its companion volume The Participatory Economy.[1] The account that follows is based primarily on the latter volume.[2]

MAIN THEORETICAL CHARACTERISTICS OF A LABOR-MANAGED ECONOMY

How the Model Works

Participation

"The Labor-managed economy is based on or composed of firms controlled and managed by those working in them. This participation in management is by all and on the basis of equality, that is, on the principle of one-man one-vote." Alternatively, each voter is given the same number of points and is allowed to assign different weights to alternative issues simultaneously to be decided upon. This participation is to be carried out through elected representative bodies and officers: a workers' council, an executive board, and the director of the firm. It should be noted that participation in control and management derives exclusively from work in the enterprise, not from participation in ownership.

Income Sharing

After paying for all costs of operation (expenditures on supplies, interest on capital, turnover tax, and other obligations) the worker-participants share equitably in the net income (total profit)

of the enterprise. Equity requires that payment be equal for labor
of equal intensity and quality, and that it be governed by a democratically agreed-on income distribution schedule. A collectively
agreed-on share of net income can be channeled into reserve funds,
collective consumption funds, and investment funds. In the last case
"it may be preferable to recognize the contributions of savings to the
firm's capital formation as individual claims of each participant,
and express them in the form of fixed interest-bearing financial obligations of the firm," such financial claims carrying, however, no
right of control or management of the firm.

Property Structure

The worker-managers do not have the full ownership of capital
assets that they use. They can enjoy the fruits of production in
which the assets were used but must pay a rental fee for this, and
they cannot destroy or sell the real assets and distribute the pro-
ceeds as current income. In turn, lenders of financial capital and
lessors of physical assets to the firm have no right of control over
the assets so long as the enterprise meets its debt-servicing obligations to them.

Other Institutional Arrangements

The labor-managed economy must be a fully decentralized
market economy. In addition to the labor-managed firms, other
decision-making units in the system (individuals, households, associations, the government) "decide freely and to their best advantage
on actions they take, without direct interference from outside. Economic planning and policy may be implemented through indirect policy instruments, discussion, improved information, or moral suasion, but never through a direct order to a firm or a group of firms."
Transactions among the various decision-making units are made
through markets, which are perfectly free whenever there are many
buyers and sellers relative to the total volume of transactions.
Where monopolistic and monopsonistic situations occur, the government may intervene, but this intervention is limited to rendering the
market structure more competitive by stimulating entry or by open-
ing up the market to international competition. The government may
also fix minimum or maximum prices in such situations. The social
preference function that emerges from such uninhibited market interaction among participants may be modified, but only through the
use of "legitimate" instruments of economic policy, such as taxes,
for example.

Employment

The labor-managed economy is characterized by freedom of employment. This means that the individual is free to take, not to take, or leave a particular job, and enterprises are free to hire or not to hire a particular worker. "However, the firms can, as a matter of their collective and democratic decision, limit in various ways their own capacity to expel a member of the community even where strictly economic considerations might call for doing so."

Claimed Advantages of the Model

The advantages claimed for the theoretical model of a labor-managed economy are the following.

Economic self-determination by all who work reduces the alienation of the worker from the product he is producing and from exploitation by managers and owners of capital. Each employee becomes part worker, part manager. He is able to control both the product he makes and the conditions of work under which he produces his share of the product. In Vanek's words, the model has the merit of avoiding the "mutilation of men when used exclusively as mechanical factors of production."

Labor management (or worker dominance) eliminates class distinctions that beset other systems. There is in it no tyranny of capitalists, corporation managers, or state bureaucrats.

A labor-managed economy, according to the model's proponents, will tend to coexist with political self-determination (democratically elected government) since workers' democracy and political democracy are mutually reinforcing. In fact, the implanting of workers' economic self-determination will, through its salutary democratic training, promote the emergence of political democracy where such is lacking.

It is also argued that "under the scrutiny of economic theory the participatory economy appears in a very favorable light, both in comparison to an absolute standard of efficiency and in comparison with other economic systems." This theoretical assessment is said to be confirmed by the empirical record of the performance of the Yugoslav worker-managed economy.

Criticism of the Model

The theoretical model of a labor-managed economy has been criticized on the following grounds:

Assuming that "the quest of men to participate in the determination and decision-making of the activities in which they are
personally involved" is really "one of the most important sociopolitical phenomena of our time," alienation in the Marxian sense
of exploitation coupled with the divorce of the worker from his product may, indeed, be attenuated in a worker-managed firm. Presumably this participation would make the workers more productive.
One could argue, however, that alienation in the Marxian sense is
not the only form of alienation. Analytically it is possible, for any
firm in the setting of competitive markets, to make a distinction between the firm as an entrepreneurial economic unit and the employees
of the firm as suppliers of labor. As an entrepreneurial economic
unit the firm will presumably seek to maximize, increase, or simply
retain its revenue. To achieve this goal it will exert internal pressure on production costs and such pressure will include an attempt
on the part of the unit to increase output per worker by, for example,
intensification of work.[3] Where workers and managers are one, it
is conceivable that a conflict between the two welded roles may arise.
In that event alienation will simply have been redefined. A subtle
attempt to shift the entrepreneurial function of the firm to the director would tend to have the effect of undoing much of the original cooperative idea.

As to the objective of classlessness, three related difficulties
are likely to present themselves: First, there will be a tendency for
the worker-managed firms to erect barriers to job entry in both the
short and the long run. The firm may be expected to try to maximize
average long-run profits per worker rather than total long-run profits,
sales, or growth. There will thus tend to be an inbuilt reluctance to
spread profits over more employees and one way of making sure
that this does not happen is to keep potential job entrants out of the
firm. In fact, it can be shown that the worker-managed firm's
short-run reaction to a price increase of its product would be to reduce the amount of the product supplied and to increase output of the
product when the price falls.[4] The propensity of worker-managed
firms to keep their doors closed may result in the firms' becoming
exclusive social clubs and to make the system a conglomerate of
such classy clubs. In the long run this tendency will be strengthened
by the role of the firm as a social and recreational center for its employees as well as by a "social constraint" that would work against
putting club members out to pasture (Vanek's power of the firm to
"limit in various ways [its] own capacity to expel a member of the
community even where strictly economic considerations might call
for doing so"). Second, within the firm, rules of seniority might
well encourage the emergence of hierarchic worker structures.
Such seniority rules are the more likely to exist where the length of

workers' tenure is considerable, as it is likely to be in worker-managed enterprises. Third, the worker-managed firms are presumed to operate in a competitive market setting. It is not unreasonable to suppose that there will develop differences in material well-being among the firms, some firms doing much better than others. In fact, in a small country (such as Yugoslavia, for example) it is conceivable that monopolistic firms will flourish in a number of sectors. In addition, therefore, to the class nature of the firms and the class structure within each firm, there will be class ranking among firms in the system. Like alienation, the class nature of society simply will be redefined.

The contention that economic self-determination will promote political democracy is questionable. The coexistence of economic self-determination with benevolent or not-so-benevolent dictatorship cannot be ruled out.

The absolute and relative efficiency of the model remains a matter of debate and dispute. We shall mention only one problem: "if technology," writes one critic of the model, "moves in the direction of substantially increasing externalities, [the model's contention that only the market is consistent with efficiency] is clearly false within the neoclassical framework which [the model] accepts."[5]

It has been suggested that the nearest thing to a fallacy of composition is to imply that a national economic system, the component enterprises of which are employee-managed, is itself thereby labor-managed. "A general economic system has its own organization, structure, regulation, properties, and operating characteristics distinct from such attributes of the entities it comprises."[6] A market economy tends to be endogenously self-regulating, not exogenously managed by, for example, workers' collectives.

Some critics have asked to what extent workers, or anybody else for that matter, are really all that anxious to participate.[7] Direct participation in allocative power connotes material risks as well as benefits and "higher" (nonmaterial) gratifications. To be directly involved takes time away from consumption and calls for a good deal of technical expertise; it not only increases self-esteem but entails a lot of heartbreak, disappointment, disillusion, and possibly financial loss. The assumption that men are inherently democratic and involved, that they possess a developed sense of social responsibility by virtue of being workers, and that they have the ability to grapple with complex technical questions or even simple repetitive administrative chores may be quite simply the projection onto others of the idiosyncratic temper of those who make the assumption. The history of humanity is in large part a record of individuals submitting with varying degrees of assent to autocratic authority: surrendering or delegating their decision-making power and, as often as not, liking it. It is argued that the phenomenon of widespread flight from choice is as true of Soviet consumers and enterprise managers as it is of stockholders and "manipulated" consumers and citizens in the West. And, the argument continues, it is not all due to the dark machinations of power-hungry elites. The qualities of individual self-assertion and social consciousness, fair play and toleration of opposing views, democratic coordination through reasoned discussion, and the instinct of equity—all these cannot be simply postulated.

WORKER PARTICIPATION IN THE YUGOSLAV ECONOMY

Ideological, Historical, and Legal Foundations

"The development of self-management in Yugoslavia has initiated in the world the process of transformation of workers into managers of their enterprises and at all levels of social organization."[8] This self-management is officially traced to the teachings of the founders of "scientific socialism": Marx, Engels, and Lenin: "Self-management in Yugoslavia represents a form of dictatorship of the proletariat. Its basic characteristic is that the working class, together with all other working people, has direct control over its working and living conditions. Self-management eliminates all intermediaries between the working class and the management of public affairs."[9] The intermediary that is particularly relevant in this context is the socialist state. After the victory of the proletariat over the bourgeoisie, workers are directly organized into associations and thus assume a hegemonic role in the promotion of socialist social relations. The state, as Marx and Engels had predicted, "withers away."[10]

The evolution of the idea and practice of workers' self-determination in Yugoslavia may be traced to two major historically determined phenomena: nationalism and the Yugoslav communist movement's guerrilla origins. Nationalism manifests itself in a stubborn spirit of independence, which in the late 1940s and early 1950s collided with Stalin's imperial ambitions. Some Western students of the Yugoslav system of workers' self-determination argue that "self-management is one of the great 'myths' of Yugoslav society, and as such it is immune to attack from within the system."[11] The myth feeds less on empirical evidence of economic success or documented social and psychological benefit than on its specific national and, originally, anti-Soviet antecedents. Any proposals for the establishment of organs of workers' self-management in the Soviet Union

or Soviet-dominated Eastern Europe, outside Yugoslavia, are likely
to bring out the tanks.[12] The guerrilla experience of the communist
movement in Yugoslavia encouraged "autochthonic socialist thinking
in Yugoslavia" to move in the direction of participatory communities
of men and to shun formalized, intermediary, hierarchic structures.
This nativism has not meant the absence of such structures or even
a very significant erosion of their political and other influence (the
League of Yugoslav Communists remains, after all, the most influential, bureaucratized body in the country; and to openly criticize Tito
is to land in jail), but it has meant organizational experimentation in
the direction of decentralization, especially economic decentralization.

The legal foundation of workers' self-determination is provided
by a series of legislative acts going back to 1950 when a law was
passed handing over the management of factories to workers. The
latest legal instruments of labor management are the 1974 Constitution of the Socialist Federal Republic of Yugoslavia and the Associated Labor Act of 1976.[13] This legislation expands the scope of self-
management to cover most social-political-economic units in Yugoslav society and emphasizes direct worker participation in management, particularly within basic units in enterprises or other decision-
making groups.

Participation

According to Vanek's general theory, the labor-managed economy is based on or composed of firms controlled and managed by
those working in them. Does this obtain in Yugoslavia? The answer
is yes, but with reservations. The bulk of industry consists of firms
in which workers have the legal right and the organizational means to
participate in management. The latest legislation extends the principle of self-determination to all kinds of decision-making units at
every level of society: to educational and cultural institutions, public health, and other spheres. Since more than one-third of the
population consists of farmers working privately owned farms, the
law, while guaranteeing "the security of private owners of agricultural land,"[14] encourages these members of the private sector to
set up joint organizations and other cooperative arrangements.[15]

The theory requires that participation be by all, on the basis
of equality (one-man one-vote), through elected representative bodies
and officers, and that it derive exclusively from work in the enterprise, not from a share in ownership. Again, legally and institutionally Yugoslav practice appears to conform to these requirements.
Within an enterprise (called "primary work organization" or "or-

ganization of associated labor") or other decision-making units (formerly referred to as "institutions") the basic organs of worker self-determination are the so-called basic organizations of associated labor (BOALs) formerly (before 1974) referred to as work units, plants, or independent departments in noneconomic organizations. A BOAL is defined as a section of the enterprise or part of the production process the product of which can be measured as a value, that is, which can be exchanged inside the enterprise or on the market.[16] According to the 1974 Constitution, the workers in the BOALs "directly and on terms of equality realize their socio-economic and other self-management rights and decide on other questions concerning their socio-economic status." By "directly" is meant via plebiscitary means, that is, through direct meetings of workers, referenda, and conferences. The questions decided on in this manner (under certain legal constraints) include improvement of methods of production and business results, income distribution, education, culture, the health service, housing construction, and the distribution of available enterprise housing among BOAL members, the services to be shared with other parts of the enterprise, what common funds there are to be, how these funds are to be administered, and what rights will be enjoyed by the workers' council of the whole enterprise.

Relationships among BOALs within an enterprise are regulated by voluntary intraenterprise "self-management agreements." These agreements, concluded directly by the parties involved, cover such items as a more rational division of labor within the enterprise (or other self-management units), pooling of resources in pursuit of common aims, and so on. "In this way the regulative and intermediary role of the state concerning relations among working people is diminished." Intraenterprise conflicts among BOALs are resolved by the enterprise trade union organization, if they cannot be resolved by regular procedures.

Associations of BOALs are entitled to delegate freely certain powers to central self-management and central administrative bodies of the enterprise. However, decisions concerning investment, collective consumption, and personal income distribution must be approved by individual BOALs. The central self-management body in an enterprise is known as a "workers' council." The central administration of an enterprise is the executive committee ("business board") of the workers' council elected by the council. In the past, depending on the size of the enterprise, the workers' council had an elected membership of workers' delegates numbering anywhere from 15 to 200. The executive committee of the workers' council (essentially a management board) had 3 to 11 members. The chairman of the executive committee (that is, the director of the enterprise) and members of the committee are selected by a procedure described as a "public competition" on the proposal of a "competition commission." This competition commission is composed of a statutorily specified number of representatives of the enterprise drawn from the workers' council, the trade unions concerned, and the local government author- ity (known as the "commune"). Members of a workers' council and members of the council's executive committee (management board) may not be elected for a period of more than two years. No one may be elected to the same workers' council or executive committee for more than two consecutive terms. Members of the executive com- mittee cannot be elected to the workers' council. The maximum tenure of the chairman of the executive committee and of the com- mittee's members is four years. After the expiration of the four years, they may be renominated for the same job by the same pro- cedures as those described above. The members of the executive committee may be relieved of office at any time by the workers' council. The chairman of the executive committee (enterprise director) has the right and duty to stay the execution of any enact- ments of the workers' council or any other body within the enter- prise if he considers such enactments to be contrary to law. In or- der to achieve and safeguard their self-management rights, workers in an enterprise or other decision-making unit have the right to ex- ercise supervision over the conduct of enterprise affairs, both directly through their various organizations (BOALs, workers' coun- cil) and through special organs of self-management workers' super- vision.

In sum, in a broad organizational chart sense, legally and in- stitutionally, Yugoslav enterprises and other noneconomic decision- making units conform to the participatory requirements of the theory of labor management as outlined in the first part of this chapter.

However, when one goes beyond the charts and legal provisions, the picture becomes more clouded. There are certain restrictions imposed on the exercise of self-management rights by workers and there exist also some less obvious but nonetheless real limitations inherent in participatory management. These various qualifications may be listed as follows:

Participation by workers in the management of their workplaces will not be effective if the worker-managers are not given all the in- formation needed to make meaningful managerial decisions. Recog- nizing this problem (that is, the tendency of professional managers to withhold information), the 1974 Constitution reiterates the obliga- tion of the chairman and members of the executive committees to supply information to the workers' council, the BOALs, and other self-management bodies. It also makes institutional provision to assure proper information flows. Nonetheless, the problem is apparently there. "Top management," says one student of the problems,

> may view participatory management by workers more
> negatively than do the workers themselves. Indeed,
> top management receives comparatively little benefit
> from workers' self-management and, moreover, they
> are more subject to the influence of the state, especially the commune. This influence, in the form of extra-
> market incentives to internalize communal objectives,
> can result in the information that flows from top to
> bottom being designed to engender decisions that are
> consistent with managerial wishes. [17]

"Under the Yugoslav system," says Holesovsky, "workers do not actually manage the firms they work for; neither do employees' representatives, delegated to a Yugoslav workers' council, take direct care of managerial duties. . . . Self-management . . . amounts to employees' delegates intervening selectively and intermittently in management, which is exercised by professional executives." [18]

Withholding or manipulating essential information is not the whole story, however. Even where information flows are satisfactory, the information must be understood by the worker-managers. This presupposes a certain minimum level of worker education. In Yugoslavia this is still a problem; much of the work force consists of recently urbanized peasants with only very modest educational qualifications. The problem is exacerbated by important regional differences in the quantity and quality of education.

Until 1974 the question of the level at which workers' control was to be exercised had not been fully resolved. The question was whether the worker should vote for his representative at the enterprise level (enterprise workers' council), or the level of his department, or plant, or at some still lower level. Should he, for example, elect his foreman, or is it technically and economically necessary to have a hierarchic structure below a certain plateau of decisions? Prior to the 1974 Constitution the Yugoslavs had experimented with semiautonomous "economic units" within the enterprise, the idea being to decentralize and debureaucratize the unwieldy workers' councils in the larger enterprises. These economic units became the BOALs of the 1974 Constitution. Nevertheless, there is reason to believe with Granick that the establishment of the BOALs did not lead to significant decentralization of key enterprise decisions. In reality the BOALs make suggestions for their own production plans (which are the building blocks of enterprise plans), [19] request information concerning plans proposed to them, and above all are concerned with what Granick calls "treatment of the individual."[20] Important decisions (for example, consumption versus investment) are delegated by the BOALs to the enterprise workers' council. However, since 1974 the BOALs have ratification powers over council decisions in such matters. While legally the workers have the right to separate their BOAL from the enterprise, they must petition—presumably the workers' council—for permission to do so. The council may reject such petition if it deems the separation to be contrary to the "collective interest" of the enterprise organization.

The institutionalization of direct worker participation in the BOALs has reduced but not eliminated another problem, which is that on important matters the workers' vote is exercised intermittently. Representatives to the workers' council are rotated every two years; managers are chosen for at least four years. This gives members of the workers' council an edge over their electorate, and the managers an edge over the council through simple durability. Moreover, worker members of the council (who serve without compensation) tend to fall into two groups: a passive and only occasionally involved majority (usually the involvement begins when it comes to dividing up the firm's net income), and an activist minority. The latter have their eyes on managerial positions and tend to identify themselves with the managerial-professional point of view. These potential managers are especially sensitive to discreet and not so discreet pressures put on them by the very permanent bureaucracies of the party and government at the factory and commune levels.

There is also a more general problem of the actual feasibility (as distinct from theoretical possibility) of fusing the managerial and labor-supplying interest and functions. Some argue that the dualism of perspectives persists, that managerial interests and the interests of workers qua workers are separate and distinct, and not complementary. These interests diverge even when workers are made to wear two hats at the same time. For example, as managers, workers will be under pressure from the banking system and "society" (governmental authorities) to maximize return on equity; as suppliers of labor who—when they leave the enterprise—can't take it (equity rights) with them, workers will be interested in maximizing return on their product while they are active in the enterprise. Although there exists a complementarity of managerial and worker functions in a narrow technical sense and agreement on that plane is realizable, there is surely still a difference in the capacity of various individuals to perform such functions. The Yugoslav argument that a workers' council or a similar body "does not represent a special sectional interest but certain interests of different groups [and that] these interests are not harmonized through 'bargaining' but through participation in decision-making,"[21] is contested by some critics. Holesovsky, for example, poses the question "whether workers' interests are better served when workers turn into their own supervisors, or when they force management indirectly, by their demands, to invest and innovate." He concludes that

> the available evidence points to the necessity, from the perspective of workers' sovereignty, to maintain an organizational dualism, even under systems of workers' self-management. The need for a specialized organ representing workers' interests is the greater the less the real weight of workers' interests in self-management organs. However, even if workers should dominate self-management organs as fully as possible, duality of point of view would not thereby disappear. In that case, too, workers' interest representation through union organizations, serving workers' control from below, would be needed.[22]

An important last point is that there is in the Yugoslav economy the very visible presence of the Communist Party and governmental bureaucracies. It will be recalled that in the selection of the executive committee (managerial board) of an enterprise, the workers have only a partial voice. The local government body, attuned to the wishes of higher-up governmental authorities (republican, federal) and to the extremely persuasive desires of the Communist Party, also has a say, perhaps the more influential one. "The designers of self-management socialism," says one Yugoslav economist, "continue to exercise parochial care over its destiny."[23] A manager in Yugoslavia has to be not merely a competent technician (his purely professional qualifications seem, in fact, to come second); he has to be, above all, a skilled politician on good terms with the local government authorities and with good pipelines to republican government and party brass. These attributes are especially important for managers of the larger enterprises.[24] The managers, in turn, influence republican and national decision making through their participation in various "chambers of commerce," "economic chambers" of republic and federal parliaments, and other sociopolitical organizations. In fact, a new and influential—as well as affluent—class of managers has come into being in Yugoslavia under the ideological umbrella of workers' self-management. Their way of life is not very different from that of managers in market-oriented and administration-oriented systems. Because of what some consider to be the myth that these managers are primarily the representatives of workers, they have to tread more gently than managers elsewhere, but not markedly so.

The general conclusion emerging under this heading of "Participation" seems to be that while it would be wrong to underplay the
reality of the drive for workers' self-management in Yugoslav enterprises (especially by comparison with enterprises in Eastern
Europe and the Soviet Union), actual autodetermination is less than
what appears on paper.

Income Sharing

Yugoslav workers' total compensation consists of two parts.
First, there is a basic wage determined essentially by the individual
worker's marginal product (payment "by results"; or as the Yugoslavs put it, "according to the contribution of each worker to the
overall development of the organization of associated labor").[25]
However, a floor is established below which no basic wage is allowed to fall: "in principle, a worker's personal income and his
other material rights must be adequate to assure him 'material and
social security and stability.'"[26] In accordance with this, some
enterprises are subsidized by the state on condition that "society
has a real interest in the survival of such organizations." This
"real interest" may be quite simply the desire to prevent the emergence of local unemployment. On the other hand, monopoly rents
accruing to other enterprises ("income which exceeds the actual results of work") are appropriated by the state. Worker collectives
have relatively little say in all this.

The second part of the Yugoslav worker's compensation consists in a share of the net revenue of the firm (BOAL, enterprise)
available for distribution as personal income. This part of total
worker compensation is roughly equivalent to capitalist profit-
sharing or dividend distribution.

The basic wage will vary considerably from firm to firm, and
from place to place, which does not conform to the theoretical model's
prescription that "equity requires that payment be equal for labor
of equal intensity and quality." The "equal stomachs" doctrine of
income distribution does not prevail in the Yugoslav enterprise, at
least not in establishing the basic wage. That wage is determined
to a considerable extent by the past technical and entrepreneurial
history of the firm and by the present and future role of these in
determining factor proportions and flows in the production process.
This approach is explicit in the Yugoslav recognition of the productivity of capital, the latter referred to as "past labor." The Marxist euphemism "past labor" is defined by the Yugoslavs as "material-
ized or objectified labor [which] ensures in practice . . . the right
[of the workers] to share in the benefits of increased productivity

achieved through the accumulation of the results of their labor over many years."[27] In other words, the structure of a BOAL and the workers' earning function within it are seen as being inseparable from the production process continuum and the BOAL's intraenterprise and interenterprise relationships.

Before sharing out the total profit (net income) among themselves, workers in the BOAL are obliged by law and the contractual commitment of their organization to subtract from the net income financial resources for public services and housing (communal consumption); capital expansion, new technology, and worker training; and the organization's reserve funds. These collective consumption, investment, and reserve deductions are not entirely or even mainly left to the direct collective decision of the workers in the BOAL. They are mandated by higher bodies ("society") in greater or lesser detail. In terms of self-determination, with respect to income distribution, Yugoslav practice thus falls short of the requirements of the labor-managed model. Here, too, as with the basic wage, there will be sizable differences among BOALs, enterprises, and regions. Hence the Yugoslav practice of income distribution departs from the theoretical model's equity requirement of equal payment for labor of equal intensity and quality. Despite the presence of group moral incentives, appeals to social consciousness, and the cooperative socialist banner on which workers' self-determination in Yugoslavia is inscribed, the incentive function of Yugoslav economic institutions remains by and large one whose main appeal is to the material interest of the individual worker.

The basic reason for compelling the worker-managed BOALs (and to an extent the enterprise workers' councils) to set aside certain resources for collective consumption, investment, and reserve is that under the system of workers' self-determination (and assuming continued adherence by worker-managers to the individual material welfare maximization ethic) there will be a tendency for the greater part of firm net income to be distributed as personal income to the workers. Since the workers' right to share in the firm's profits depends exclusively on the workers' active participation in the work of the BOAL/enterprise, the temptation to distribute profit now (while one is still around) will be very strong. Reinvested, the profits may, indeed, give rise to higher productivity and a larger income stream in the future, but perhaps only after the present worker-managers leave the firm. Once they leave, any rights they had to a share of the firm's net income automatically cease. Hence the possibility of underinvestment ("share-out all") in a system of workers' management. Hence also the statutory rules regarding the priority claims of investment, reserve, and collective consumption; rules that restrict the scope of workers' self-determination.

Property Structure

The property structure of the Yugoslav worker-managed firm fulfills the requirements of the labor-managed economy model. The Yugoslav firm has the unattenuated right of ownership in its earnings, and usus fructus rights in capital goods ("past labor"), the attenuated ownership of the latter being vested in "society," that is, the state.[28] In other words, the worker-managers are legally entitled to enjoy the fruits of production in which the assets of the firm are used, but they must pay a rental fee (interest charge) for this right. They can buy and sell capital goods but are obliged to maintain the book value of the assets through depreciation or the reinvestment of the monies obtained from sale of the assets. If the firm should sell an asset at less than its book value, it has to deduct the difference from its earnings and reinvest that difference.

Other Institutional Arrangements

It will be recalled that "other institutional arrangements" refer to the extraenterprise institutional structure of the economy, the theoretical requirement being that this be a fully decentralized market-type structure, with governmental intervention made through indirect ("legitimate" in a market sense) instruments of policy, not through direct orders to firms.

The Yugoslav economy may be regarded as a quite imperfectly competitive market economy with three important qualifications. First, there exist concentrations of economic power, that is, strong pressures moving the economy toward the monopolistic competition end of the market spectrum. For example, in 1971, the largest 79 manufacturing and mining enterprises accounted for 53.4 percent of the sales, 47.6 percent of the assets, and 37 percent of the employment in the manufacturing sector. Second, the economy contains elements of central administration, which means that governmental intervention is not limited to "legitimate" instruments of policy, but includes direct orders to specific firms or groups of firms. This type of direct ("administrative") intervention, which bypasses or ignores market signals, consists of governmental investments in designated priority sectors (including projects intended to reduce regional developmental inequalities),[29] regulation of private-sector activities, and of foreign exchange. Despite resort to administrative means of policy, and the drift—since the early 1970s—away from purely market solutions to economic problems, it is correct to say that governmental intervention in the economy is primarily ad hoc, emphasizing monetary and fiscal measures. It seeks to alter the market param-

eters within which individual firms and other units make their decisions, not to totally supplant these parameters. Yugoslav planning
has been by and large "indicative," that is, "guiding" rather than
constraining. The plans provide general information about social
objectives preferred by the government, with the suggestion that
these be incorporated in the plans of the individual decision-making
units. Third, since 1974 emphasis has been given to a socialist
system of "social compacts." The stated purpose of these is both
to reduce the direct and indirect role of the state in the resolution
of economic problems, such as the enforcement of an incomes or
price control policy, and gradually to replace market forces in economic decision making. The compacts on specific questions of economic policy are concluded between government authorities, trade
unions, "chambers of the economy," and enterprises (or other sociopolitical organizations) and among enterprises in a given industrial
branch. Shorn of its self-management mystique, the compacts seem
to amount to something one could describe as interfirm cartel arrangements. Their intrafirm equivalents are the "self-management
agreements" referred to earlier.

Employment

The system of workers' self-management creates a number
of employment problems directly traceable to the attempt made by
the worker-managed firms to maximize long-term income per participant and the socialist principle of not firing workers except for
very serious cause. The attempt to maximize long-term income
per member of the firm collective while not firing anybody means
that the firm will not hire an additional worker unless his marginal
product is well above the average product of all presently employed
workers in the firm.[30] Moreover, workers in BOALs and enterprises that are doing well are reluctant to change jobs since a movement to another firm means the loss of usufruct rights to profits in
the present firm. Several consequences follow. Labor mobility is
low, averaging about 1 percent of the labor force in the 1960s. Because of the barriers erected by firms to new entrants, unemployment is high (9.1 percent in 1968; never falling below 7.2 percent
through 1972), and there is a tendency toward wrong factor proportions: understaffing a capital equipment in the better-off firms,
the opposite in the weak firms, the latter kept afloat by government
subsidies. The low labor mobility makes it difficult to reduce interfirm income inequalities.

CONCLUSION

The Yugoslav economy is, indeed, the nearest available empirical approximation to the theoretical model of a labor-managed economy. In practice, workers' self-determination is not as full as the model prescribes, and the advantages are not as pure and evident as the proponents of the model predicted. The Yugoslav economy has suffered from unemployment, low labor mobility, sharp income inequalities, and other problems. The question as to the extent to which alienation has been reduced remains and the answers are highly subjective. Some go so far as to argue that the still modest level of Yugoslavia's economic development, and that country's uncertain future as a cohesive national entity, make it quite unlikely that the Yugoslav variant of workers' self-management will exert much influence on other, especially the more advanced, countries. Indeed, the very survival of the system of workers' participation in the Yugoslav form is put to question.[31] Others see in the Yugoslav experiment a promise of man's liberation that, with appropriate adjustments, could be generalized and made to work in other societies.

NOTES

1. Both books published by Cornell University Press (Ithaca, N.Y.: 1970, 1971). See also J. Vanek, ed., Self-Management: Economic Liberation of Man (Harmondsworth: Penguin, 1975), and J. Vanek, "The Yugoslav Economy Viewed Through the Theory of Labor Management," World Development 1, no. 9 (September 1973): 39-56. A somewhat different approach is taken by B. Horvat in his "Prilog zasnivanju teorije jugoslavenskog poduzeca" ("Contribution to the Establishment of a Theory of the Yugoslav Enterprise"), Ekonomska Analiza, Nos. 1-2 (1976), pp. 7-28.

2. All quotations not marked with a footnote number are from that volume.

3. This point is made by Vaclav Holesovsky in his review of Vanek's The Participatory Economy in Journal of Economic Issues 7, no. 1 (March 1973): 100.

4. R. L. Carson, Comparative Economic Systems (New York: Macmillan, 1973), pp. 623-28.

5. Benjamin Ward, review of Vanek's The Participatory Economy in Journal of Economic Issues 7, no. 1 (March 1973): 97.

6. P. E. Koefod, review of Vanek's The Participatory Economy in Journal of Economic Issues 10, no. 4 (December 1972): 1222.

7. An attempt to measure the intensity of worker participation in enterprise decision making under Yugoslav conditions may be found in Josip Obradovic, Workers' Participation in Yugoslavia: Theory and Research (Columbia: Institute of International Studies, University of South Carolina, Occasional Paper, n.d.).

8. Rados Smiljkovic, Workers' Self-Management in Yugoslavia (Belgrade: Federal Committee for Information, n.d.), p. 28.

9. Ibid., p. 7.

10. "The essence of self-management by workers in Yugoslavia is not the participation of workers in decision-making on public affairs, but their direct decision-making—free from any intermediaries." Ibid., p. 14.

11. David Granick, cited by Vaclav Holesovsky, Economic Systems: Analysis and Comparison (New York: McGraw-Hill, 1977), p. 452.

12. The Yugoslavs officially deny this. "A popular theme of Western political literature is that the Yugoslav system of socialist self-management came into existence as a consequence of the dispute between the Communist Party of Yugoslavia and Stalin. Undoubtedly, the dispute with Stalin encouraged the development of self-management, but it did not occasion it. The roots of self-management lie in Marxist-Leninist ideology, in autochthonic socialist thinking in Yugoslavia, and in the very character of her socialist revolution at the core of which was the working class led by the Communist Party." Smiljkovic, op. cit., p. 9.

13. The Constitution of the Socialist Federal Republic of Yugoslavia (New York: Cross-Cultural Communications, Merrick, 1976); The Associated Labour Act (Belgrade: Secretariat of Information of the SFR Yugoslavia Assembly, 1976).

14. But only "on condition that they adjust their methods of work to the prevailing overall socio-economic conditions" in Yugoslavia. Smiljkovic, op. cit., p. 26.

15. A self-employed person may associate his labor and pool his resources with others solely on a self-management basis. He sets up with them a contractual work organization in which he has the right to be manager. The others have the same self-management rights as those employed in organizations whose means of work are social property. . . . The Constitution leaves scope for employment outside the socially owned sector even beyond the framework of a contractual organization. Self-employed persons may employ a limited number of persons. In such cases the trade unions and associations representing both parties appear on the

> scene and a contract is concluded specifying the
> duties of each party.

Ibid., p. 27, and Article 68 of the 1974 Constitution, op. cit., p. 51. In industry, five is the "limited number" of people a self-employed person may employ without forming a contractual organization of associated labor.

16. Another way of defining a BOAL is as a component part of an organization of associated labor (enterprise, institution) that makes up a technologically rounded whole, an independent economic and self-managing unit, which can have the character of a legal entity. These correspond to the former "economic units" that were independent self-management organizations within an enterprise with much the same decision-making powers as the BOALs. See Laura D'Andrea Tyson, "The Yugoslav Economy in the 1970's: A Survey of Recent Developments and Future Prospects," in East European Economies Post-Helsinki, A Compendium of Papers Submitted to the Joint Economic Committee, Congress of the United States (Washington, D.C.: U.S. Government Printing Office, 1977), p. 948ff.

17. John F. Schnell, "An Inquiry into the Nature of the Yugoslav Labor-Managed Enterprise in Light of the Institution of Basic Organizations of Associated Labor" (Unpublished graduate paper, Department of Economics, Pennsylvania State University, November 1977).

18. Holesovsky, Economic Systems, op. cit., pp. 452–53.

19. Since 1976 the nationwide planning system is to be from the bottom up. Individual plans originating within the enterprise are coordinated into an enterprise plan. Enterprise plans are aggregated and reconciled by republican and federal authorities into a national plan. All enterprise plans must be drafted in conformity with a common methodology, common assumptions, and a common plan period. Tyson, op. cit., p. 950.

20. David Granick, Enterprise Guidance in Eastern Europe: A Comparison of Four Socialist Countries (Princeton, N.J.: Princeton University Press, 1975), pp. 377–78. See also Josip Obradovic, "Workers' Participation: Who Participates," Industrial Relations 14, no. 1 (February 1975): 32–44. "Treatment of the individual" covers matters such as providing group incentive pay for members of the BOAL in conformity with the production and productivity plan, and in distributing personal income and enterprise housing among members.

21. Josip Zupanov, "The Yugoslav Enterprise," in Comparative Economic Systems: Models and Cases, ed. Morris Bornstein, 3d ed. (Homewood, Ill.: Irwin, 1974), p. 185.

22. Holesovsky, Economic Systems, op. cit., pp. 452, 457.

23. Aleksander Bajt, "Management in Yugoslavia," in Bornstein, op. cit., p. 197.

24. Managers have been fired by the government without consulting of the workers' councils.

25. "A worker receives an income which is commensurate to his contribution to the earnings from sales on the market." Smiljkovic, op. cit., p. 17. Schnell (op. cit., p. 10) notes that "based on 'units of labor intensity' in one Serbian enterprise, the ratio of the simplest to the most complex work is 1:9, but based on a 'formula of solidarity,' the ratio between the lowest and the highest basic income is 1:5."

26. Smiljkovic, op. cit., p. 17.

27. Constitution of the SFRY, op. cit., Glossary of Terms, pp. 164-65. See also E. Kardelj, "The Organizing of Associated Labor Along Self-Management Lines," Socialist Thought and Practice: A Yugoslav Monthly 15, no. 1 (January 1975): 3-43 (especially p. 11).

28. The economics of property rights both as a theoretical construct and empirical (Yugoslav) application has been examined by S. Pejovich and E. Furubotn in a number of essays. For example, "Property Rights, Economic Decentralization, and the Evolution of the Yugoslav Firm, 1965-1972," Journal of Law and Economics 16, no. 2 (October 1973): 275-302. The authors define property rights as "codified relations among men arising from a very existence of and pertaining to the use of things." These rights "specify the principles of behavior with respect to things which each and every person in his daily interaction with other persons must observe." The "right of ownership" (whether private or public) is defined by two fundamental characteristics: exclusivity of right to use a thing or service, and voluntary transferability of that right. In practice the right of ownership is always "attenuated," that is, some restrictions are placed on either or both characteristics.

29. Government investment represented 17 percent of total fixed investment expenditures in the Yugoslav economy in 1970-1975. Investment by the socialized banking system (another way for the state to influence firm decisions) represented just under 50 percent of total fixed investment at that time.

30. Egon Neuberger and William Duffy, Comparative Economic Systems: A Decision-Making Approach (Boston: Allyn and Bacon, 1976), Chapter 15, "Yugoslavia," pp. 252-53. See also Carmelo Mesa-Lago, "Unemployment in a Socialist Economy: Yugoslavia," Industrial Relations 10, no. 1 (February 1971): 49-69.

31. For example, Wayne E. Leeman, Centralized and Decentralized Economic Systems (Chicago: Rand McNally, 1977), pp. 174-75.

5
EPILOGUE

The primitive Stalinist Soviet-type economy was an instrument of mass mobilization of resources. Its first purpose was to generate rapid growth of output by battering the developmental problem with comparatively unimproved production factors. The purpose was attained, but at rising factor cost. At the time of Stalin's death the economy was suffering from static misallocations of resources, sectoral imbalances, deteriorating capital performance, sluggish increases in labor productivity, low yields per acre, deficient incentives, consumer unrest, and other ills. These began to affect adversely the growth rate and, therefore, received the attention of the leadership. A similar situation came to light in China after the death of Mao.

A basic problem was that the primitive Soviet-type economy made no institutional provision for monitoring quality in the broadest sense. It had no systemic sensors that would detect waste and inefficiency, nor did it possess a mechanism whereby the detected waste and inefficiency would be automatically corrected. In fact, the largely physical-administrative means used by the center to plan the economy both in its broad sweep and its infinite detail did not even assure internal consistency of the allocative decisions that were made. The economy, it was agreed, was overcentralized (the central planners took on too many jobs), the information system was deficient (physical commands were too numerous, equivocal, contradictory, and difficult to enforce, and the reverse flow of information to the planners was a pack of lies much of the time), coordination was lax, and the incentive system was crippled, especially in the collectivized countryside, but elsewhere too.

The attention of the reformers centered on the relationship between the planning authorities and the executors of the planners' commands (especially enterprise managements), and on the instruments used by the economy to formulate preferences, disseminate information, coordinate decisions, and motivate workers and managers. Similar concerns were expressed in China some two decades later after the death of Mao.

As regards the center's relationship to the system's periphery, there was a fair measure of agreement that the decision-making process had to be decentralized. In the setting of a centrally planned administrative command economy decentralization can be two quite different things. It may be "administrative" or "economic." Administrative decentralization means that the existing system of administrative orders remains by and large intact, but now some decisions—usually the relatively small ones—are made at lower levels of the administrative hierarchy. For example, the decision to import a particular good, instead of being made by the Ministry of Foreign Trade, is now taken by the branch ministry directly concerned with the product. Decisions formerly made by one bureau at a high level are now made by six bureaus at lower levels. A shoe factory is still told by its superiors to produce shoes, but it is no longer forced to produce brown shoes only. Administrative decentralization leaves untouched the vertical structure of the command economy, its upward flow of data and downward flow of orders. The planners' right to plan and directly enforce both macro magnitudes and micro detail is not challenged. The question is merely how much burdensome detail handled at the top should be delegated to planning organs lower down the pyramid.

The decision to preserve hierarchic prerogatives, but spread the burden over the larger planning family, naturally affects the reform of planning instruments. Since households and enterprise managements do not become independent competing nodes of decision-making power, prices within the administratively decentralized system will not signal relative utilities and resource costs. With respect to the instruments of information, coordination, and incentive administration, decentralization merely aims to do two things: reduce the number of physical (or technical coefficient) indicators issued by the planners to enterprises and concentrate on the "better" ones (the ones more nearly concerned with factor quality) as, for example, indicators of labor productivity and capital/output ratios; and have greater recourse to financial ("value") indicators like prices, wages, profits, interest rates, and differential rents, after improving the cost accounting procedures used in fixing them. Administrative decentralization of a command economy will usually go through a mammoth recalculation of prices and tariff wages but will not allow the recalculated prices and wages to be set thereafter by anyone other than the planners. The newly important financial indicators are only partly "synthetic" in that they sum up more than one dimension of the allocative problem, but they are not fully "synthetic" in the sense of conveying opportunity cost information.

An administratively decentralized command system thus remains organically very close to its predecessor. Like its parent, it is short on dynamic efficiency and unable in practice to determine optimality of resource allocating choices. The central kitchen, so to speak, is extended over several floors and there are more cooks; but the ingredients are the same and so is the soup.

The post-Stalin Soviet reforms were of the administrative decentralization variety. They improved parts of the old engine and caused new problems in other parts. They did not, however, change the system in any fundamental respect. The Soviet reforms, like those of Poland, East Germany, Bulgaria, Romania, and—in the end—Czechoslovakia, were changes within, not of, the system; systemic repairs, not system replacements. If one accepts the definition of economic modernization as covering more than levels of technology, factor productivity, pace of innovation, and capital endowment per worker, and as including behavioral attributes such as democratization of human relations and respect for user wants, then the Soviet reforms made little if any dent in the problem. Even in the narrower first meaning of modernization, the old disabilities persist: the bottlenecks, the misallocations, the unfinished and unfinishable investment projects, the sluggishness of grassroots innovation, the lags in embodying inventions in production and in dumping obsolete methods, the continued tutelage exercised over enterprise managements, workers, and consumers by arrogant, often ignorant planners (the "they" as distinct from the "us" in Russian everyday parlance), and the hoarding and consequent underemployment of labor and capital caused by the ratchet principle of planning. All these disabilities put to question the official statistics witnessing to improvements in factor productivity and the human quality of the system.

Economic decentralization of an administrative command system is different. Like its administrative counterpart, it is concerned with two issues: the relationship between the central government and the system's economic units, and the instruments of goal formulation, information, coordination, and incentive. However, economic decentralization offers answers that are very different from those supplied by administrative decentralization.

Economic decentralization redistributes decision-making power among the participants in the system, not just among members of the governmental planning establishment. It gives individual economic units the capacity to formulate their own objectives

in line with their perception of the costs and benefits involved in
commercial transactions freely entered into. Vertical information
flows are replaced by horizontal contracts, and coordination through
price and the competitive striving of economic units takes the place
of mandatory linkages established by administrative command. Put
in a different way, the plan emerges from the free interaction of
buyers and sellers rather than buyer-seller contracts being entered
into in conformity with a centrally predetermined and compulsory
plan.

While physical instruments of information and coordination
are not completely dispensed with, the principal information-
coordination-incentive mechanism consists of market prices that
indicate to the decision-making participants the relative resource
costs and utilities within the system. The participants adapt their
actions to the price signals according to their perception of their
own material interest. Governmental intervention in the economy
is primarily of an indirect guiding type. It uses first and foremost
monetary and fiscal means to make its guidance felt. Intervention
is directed primarily at the economy's macro magnitudes; detailed
micro intervention is the exception. The Soviet economic reforms
of the 1960s never got that far. The Hungarian reforms did, but
hesitantly and partially.

The Hungarian and Yugoslav reforms represent virtually the
only attempts at socialist systemic reform that were actually implemented. China's Maoist arrangements were "left" administrative reforms. The famous Chinese decentralization after 1957 was
essentially administrative. Maoist preoccupation with equity of
income distribution (leveling down) and disciplining the bureaucrats
(redistribution of administrative power income) represented shifts
of emphasis rather than radical alterations of the Soviet-type system. They were jettisoned very quickly after the death of Mao.
Even the introduction of worker participation in enterprise management through revolutionary committees and other three-way combinations (now discarded) was an administrative move that did not
alter the vertical structure of both the enterprises and the system
as a whole. The revolutionary committees became "democratic"
not because they were designed to be so, but because of the bitter
factionalism that prevailed during and after the Cultural Revolution.
Maoism was not an alternative economic system, but rather a particular facade of a Soviet-type edifice. There is not much left of it
anymore, although it could be put back in place if China's present
course does not yield the expected dividends in modernization and
improvements in the material condition of the masses.

Economic decentralization meets with opposition from various
quarters, including the planning establishment and some managers

who have grown accustomed to the existing system and, indeed, personally benefit from the way the system works. The Hungarian experience also shows that there are conceptual constraints on the extent and thoroughness of any reform. They include the principle of full employment, price stability, below equilibrium pricing of basic necessities, and the immortality of firms. The Hungarian reform was halted more because of workers' fear of unemployment and consumers' fear of rising prices than because of any signs of displeasure shown by Moscow. So far only the Yugoslavs have been willing to ignore these constraints.

What emerges from this review of the issues involved in socialist economic modernization is that the contemporary Soviet-type economy, being an administratively somewhat decentralized version of the Stalinist administrative command model, has not really tackled the systemic obstacles to modernization inherent in Stalinism. The contemporary Soviet-type economy continues to subscribe to the belief that the state—meaning the party and governmental bureaucracies—knows better than everyone else what is best for society and for the individual. So long as this dictatorial view of life is alive, economic modernization will be hamstrung by feudal attitudes. The possibility is unlikely that a Communist Party in power will voluntarily abandon this philosophical position and vest the individual person and microeconomic groups with the rights and responsibilities of decision making. Even in Yugoslavia the monopoly political position of the party remains unchallengeable.

BIBLIOGRPHY

Abouchar, Alan, ed. The Socialist Price Mechanism. Durham: Duke University Press, 1977.

Adides, Ichak. Industrial Democracy: Yugoslav Style. New York: Free Press, 1972.

Bornstein, Morris, ed. Plan and Market. New Haven, Conn.: Yale University Press, 1973.

_____. Economic Planning, East and West. Cambridge, Mass.: Ballinger, 1975.

Brown, Alan, and Egon Neuberger. International Trade and Central Planning. Berkeley: University of California Press, 1968.

Brus, Wlodzimierz. The Market in a Socialist Economy. London: Routledge, 1972.

Campbell, Robert. The Soviet-Type Economies: Performance and Evolution. Boston: Houghton Mifflin, 1974.

Dorfman, Robert. The Price System. Englewood Cliffs, N.J.: Prentice-Hall, 1964.

Eckstein, Alexander, ed. Comparison of Economic Systems: Theoretical and Methodological Approaches. Berkeley: University of California Press, 1971.

Ellman, Michael. Soviet Planning Today: Proposals for an Optimally Functioning Economic System. Cambridge: Cambridge University Press, 1971.

_____. Planning Problems in the USSR: The Contribution of Mathematical Economics to Their Solution. Cambridge: Cambridge University Press, 1973.

Fallenbuchl, Zbigniew, ed. Economic Development in the Soviet Union and Eastern Europe. Vol. 1: Reforms, Technology, and Income Distribution. New York: Praeger, 1975.

Friss, István, ed. Reform of the Economic Mechanism in Hungary. Budapest: Akadémiai Kiadó, 1969.

Granick, David. Enterprise Guidance in Eastern Europe. Princeton, N.J.: Princeton University Press, 1976.

Grossman, Gregory, ed. Money and Plan: Financial Aspects of East European Economic Reforms. Berkeley: University of California Press, 1968.

Horchler, Gabriel F. Hungarian Economic Reforms: A Selective Partially Annotated Bibliography. New Brunswick, N.J.: Hungarian Research Center, 1977.

Horvat, Branko. The Yugoslav Economic System. White Plains, N.Y.: M. E. Sharpe, 1980.

Horvat, Branko, M. Markovic, and R. Supek. Self-Governing Socialism. White Plains, N.Y.: M. E. Sharpe, 1980.

Kaser, Michael, and Richard Portes, eds. Planning and Market Relations. London: Macmillan, 1971.

Liu, Guoguang, and Zhao Renwei. "Socialist Economic Planning and the Market." Peking Review, August 3, 1979, pp. 8-12.

Nove, Alec. The Soviet Economic System. London: George Allen and Unwin, 1977.

Okun, Arthur. Equality and Efficiency: The Big Tradeoff. Washington, D.C.: Brookings Institution, 1975.

Pejovich, Svetozac, ed. The Codetermination Movement in the West. Lexington, Mass.: Lexington Books, 1978.

Prybyla, Jan. The Chinese Economy: Problems and Policies. Columbia: University of South Carolina Press, 1978, 1980.

Román, Z., ed. Progress and Planning in Industry. Budapest: Akádemiai Kiadó, 1972.

Rosovsky, Henry, ed. Industrialization in Two Systems: Essays in Honor of Alexander Gerschenkron. New York: Wiley, 1966.

Šik, Ota. Plan and Market Under Socialism. White Plains, N.Y.: International Arts and Sciences Press, 1967.

Spulber, Nicolas. Socialist Management and Planning: Topics in Comparative Socialist Economics. Bloomington: Indiana University Press, 1971.

Thornton, Judith, ed. Economic Analysis of the Soviet-Type System. Cambridge: Cambridge University Press, 1976.

Vanek, Jaroslav. The General Theory of Labor Managed Market Economies. Ithaca: Cornell University Press, 1970.

_____. The Participatory Economy. Ithaca: Cornell University Press, 1971.

Ward, Benjamin. The Socialist Economy: A Study of Organizational Alternatives. New York: Rnadom House, 1967.

Weitzman, Martin L. "The New Soviet Incentive Model." Bell Journal of Economics 7, no. 1 (Spring 1976): 251-57.

Wilczynski, J. The Economics of Socialism. Chicago: Aldine, 1970.

Xue, Muqiao. "A Study in the Planned Management of the Socialist Economy." Peking Review, October 26, 1979, pp. 14-20.

INDEX

Vanek, Jaroslav, 87, 89, 91, 93, 95, 106
Vietnam, 1

wages, ix, 1, 7, 19, 25, 41, 42, 45-47, 53, 58-62, 65, 67, 68-69, 83-84, 88, 89, 102ff, 111
Ward, Benjamin, 106
Watstein, Joseph, 36
Weitzman, M. L., 37
Wesson, Robert, 37
Western democracies, 13, 25, 32, 45, 55, 92, 73-74, 94
West Germany, 51, 88
Wilczynski, J., 35
work conditions, viii-ix, 2, 45, 46, 48, 56, 59-62, 79-80, 83, 88

worker participation, ix-x, 15, 34, 44, 48, 56-59, 88-89, 91-94ff, 112; trade unions, 17, 19, 46, 56, 104, 107; workers councils, 15, 17, 19, 24, 44, 59, 70, 73, 89-90, 96ff, 106-08

Yugoslavia, vii-x, 4, 15, 17, 19, 24, 39, 65, 70-71, 91ff, 111-13; basic organizations of associated labor (BOALs), 96ff, 102ff, 104 106-07

Zhou Enlai, 40
Zupanov, Josip, 108

ABOUT THE AUTHOR

JAN S. PRYBYLA is professor of economics at the Pennsylvania State University. He is the author of <u>The Political Economy of Communist China</u> (1970) and <u>The Chinese Economy: Problems and Policies</u> (1978; 2nd rev. edition 1980).